# RETURN TICKET PLEASE

Derek Williams

ATHENA PRESS
LONDON

RETURN TICKET PLEASE
Copyright © Derek Williams

All Rights Reserved

No part of this book may be reproduced in any form
by photocopying or by any electronic or mechanical means,
including information storage or retrieval systems,
without permission in writing from both the copyright
owner and the publisher of this book.

ISBN 1 84401 458 4

First Published in 2005 by
ATHENA PRESS
Queen's House, 2 Holly Road
Twickenham TW1 4EG
United Kingdom

Printed for Athena Press

RETURN TICKET PLEASE

## ACKNOWLEDGEMENTS

Many and special thanks to the people who have helped, and been through this experience with me. Thanks to the staff at the neurological department in Southampton and the nurses and doctors on Woodford and Farley Wards at Salisbury District Hospital. A special thank you to Jo Gibson and Dr Walters, of Nunton Ward, and an extra special thank you to my lovely wife, Deb, who not only stood by and supported me through this, but also provided the title for this book. Thanks, my love. I love you.

## CHAPTER
## One

HI, MY NAME is Derek Williams. I am thirty-two years old. Let me tell you a bit about me. Up until seven months ago, I was living, I suppose, a normal life: going to work, having a laugh at work, coming home from work, meeting my girlfriend (now my wife), Debby, or meeting my mates for a few bevvies.

But that all changed when one early morning in March, I had a brain haemorrhage, or to use the medical term, a stroke. Now you may think thirty-two is very young to have a stroke. Well it is, but I had a dark secret. I was, and still am, an alcoholic, although now I am a recovering alcoholic. I say secret because unbeknown to Debby, my family and my closest friends, I was drinking myself to death. I know there have been, and are, loads of people who this has happened to and is happening to: I do not presume myself to be unique. I am writing this, firstly to learn about computers, and secondly to give my left arm some much needed exercise. The reason that my left arm is so weak is that the stroke affected the right side of my brain, thus disabling the left side of my body. A quick and easy definition of stroke is that it's like a heart attack but in the brain.

Back to my drinking. Well, as most people, I enjoyed going to the pub, having a few pints, a few games of pool or darts and a general good crack. Oh, and mustn't forget the cheeseburger with mushrooms, as my body needed some real food inside it, not just the God knows how many pints, litres, gallons of alcohol I consumed. You can never really pinpoint the time you become an alcoholic or why. Some say it's hereditary; maybe. Some say it's because of an abused upbringing; could be, but my own humble opinion is that it's the result of boredom. You find that what you are doing in your life has become so stale, that you get an 'I can do this with my eyes shut' attitude and you have to find a stimulus to increase your appetite for life. You may say, 'Well, go and find something more challenging to do,' which many people do, and I applaud them, but this is my own account of how the Devil got hold of me and refused to let go until He almost destroyed me.

Christmas time is probably when we have our first encounter with the Prince of Darkness. There'll be Dot and Frank, Nan and Gramps giving us our first little taster. Now this may sound like a stupid theory, but I think even as young as we were, our first taste of alcohol has sown the seeds in our brain, registering in the most powerful computer in the world that this is something it likes. Yes, I know obviously that at that tender and innocent age, we can't nip into the offy for our fix and get two cans of super-strength cider, hoping and praying that someone we know doesn't come in, so as to expose our secret, then getting a private place to down the quickest cans you'll probably see (one of my many was the bus station toilets), disposing of your evidence and carrying on with your day safe in the knowledge that *He* is inside you to keep you going till next meal time.

So what's being so young and having a Christmas time

mouthful of alcohol got to do with turning into an alcoholic? Basically, it's there inside us as we develop more and learn new things. I believe the brain says, 'Hold on, I want to go back to that thing I had all those years ago,' as it's getting fed. As we all know, the more tolerant it becomes, the more it needs. That's where problems occur.

When I sum up my family and alcohol, Frank and Dot have always been quite heavy drinkers. Nothing to my extent, but quite heavy. Whereas my brother very, very rarely drinks, and I can remember him when we were younger, always refusing that little smidgen of drink whereas I was always first in the queue. Again, to me this confirms my suspicions that some of us are destined to be alcoholics. Would it have been different if it were my brother and not me who had been so eager to taste the Devil's urine?

# CHAPTER
# Two

WELL, THESE ARE just my own personal views on how I, and others, may become alcoholics. Even though alcohol has done my brain who knows what damage, it's surprising the many details I can remember about my life. It's definitely a staggered process to become an alcoholic. I do remember when I was seventeen-ish, which was the first time I could get alcohol for nothing and without being sneaky, but we'll come back to that. I say without being sneaky, because that is how I was behaving from as young as twelve. Now you may get people saying, 'Twelve years old? I was nine when I started drinking!' But you must understand I'm not trying to glorify what I became, whereas a lot of these people have not been taken in by Satan's charms! These are people who don't truly know what it's like to have 'Him' as your best friend and are just trying to look big. More of that later as well.

For now, alcohol started to enter more and more into my life. Frank used to make his home-made beer and wine and there was always a bottle of whisky in the drinks cabinet for whatever reason. When he and Dot were out, I would take it upon myself to lighten their load a little bit. This is when that first drink as a nipper was jogging my brain to not miss out on such a golden opportunity to feed. It was a simple procedure at first, then a bit riskier later. I started off with just the beer and a tiny bit of whisky at first. Frank used to get 1-litre bottles and 1½-litre bottles out of his container of home brew. I'm not really a bitter drinker, but it was free and gave me the desired effect I wanted; not needed at that time, just wanted. It was OK to taste, not blow your brains out stuff that some kids' dads would make – you know, the stuff that would literally peel the paint from the walls.

Anyway, the best days for me to 'dance with the Devil was on a Tuesday or a Saturday. Tuesday = Frank at work, Dot doing the weekly shopping; Saturday = both of them in town. My plan of procedure was a simple one, certainly not complicated, because if I was caught, I was dead. So as soon as Dot toddled off into town, my procedure burst into action. Firstly the curtains would be closed; didn't want any uninvited guests at our party. This was our party; Lucifer's and mine. Then I would grab a glass from the cabinet; didn't matter which one they all had my name on. A quick nip to the kitchen to grab a glass jar. 'What the hell do you want a glass jar for?' you may ask. Well, the glass jar is full of cold water. If I'm taking beer out, no matter how small the amount, I'm replacing it with some form of liquid. Oh, and of course we can't forget the tea towel to mop up any spillages, which did occur from time to time, but thankfully nothing major like a whole bottle. Now that would have taken some explaining.

So, now we have our equipment. At first we didn't want to take the piss and get caught, so we just took a little bit from the 1-litre bottles, thinking it best to leave the 1½-litre and half ones as they had different lids. Out of the sixteen bottles I would take a tiny swig from about ten, just to make sure none were diluted too much.

Now the beer is done, put the bottles back in the cabinet properly, as Frank would have noticed an ant's leg on them from fifty metres if someone had been tampering with his beloved. Now the whisky! Sometimes there was only a tot of this left. When there was, it was a case of don't touch – way too risky! But most of the time there was a decent enough amount left to be safe. We'll move on later to a few more risks I've taken over the years. Now we have our concoction, which would have come to just under ½ a pint. May not sound a lot, but to a twelve-year-old, it's like you're the best in the world at anything now He's been consumed. Now it's a very thorough cleaning and drying of the glass and a double and treble check to make sure everything is how it was before your little escapade. That completed, it's off to school on Tuesdays or off to see your mates Saturday. Like I said, half a pint isn't a lot, but at twelve when you're experimenting, you don't think those little ½ pints are going to make you an alcoholic but your brain knows! Your brain is remembering that little imp of a taste that Christmas time, all them years ago.

To set the record straight, this didn't happen every Tuesday and Saturday – blimey, no – but often enough to keep the brain interested for future years to come. So now I've got my little set-up on some Tuesdays. Tuesdays would be looked forward to some weeks; other weeks it was just the same old Tuesday...

You never know how your breath smells after drinking alcohol, but even at school my breath was noticed – not by a teacher thankfully, but a couple of pupils did comment on my breath. One I'll always remember. A boy called James Riley noticed one day as we were lined up waiting to go into a tutorial. Bless him; he thought I'd had bacon and eggs for breakfast. I just agreed with him, knowing I was enjoying the high with my Friend. Let's face it, a first-year pupil at secondary school certainly isn't going to think one of his classmates has just gulped down a concoction of beer and whiskey!

So here we have a normal twelve-year-old kid, drinking, not every day, but obviously enough to light up the spark in his brain. The Devil is having his starter. He's still hungry, and wants his main course, dessert, cheese and biscuits, and coffee with his After Eight mints, but he doesn't want to pay the bill. That's down to me, and believe me, it was an expensive meal.

As I have said, no one knows when they become an alcoholic. It never bothered me. I was doing this occasionally at twelve years old. I was only twelve; I was experimenting as all twelve-year-old children do. Some may do Judo, Karate, go to Scouts and so on; just happens mine was alcohol. As I've said, I'm not trying to glamorise being an alcoholic, and I apologise to anyone this may offend, but this is a no bullshit, no holds barred account of me, Derek Williams, the alcoholic. Other alcoholics' stories will be different, plus – I never thought I'd say this – but in the computer, I think I've found a new addiction.

Well, Saturday, as I've said, was another day occasionally reserved for Beelzebub and me. Dot and Frank would go down the Club for a couple of hours for their own little drink, ignorant of the fact that their young offspring was joining them in his own little way. Saturdays would follow the same procedure as Tuesdays, but now there would be people around with a little more experience than a twelve-year-old boy who thought you had just eaten bacon and eggs: now you had two experienced drinkers who may just have a slight inkling you'd been drinking. So you have to act as normal as possible, despite the fact that you know, and are under the influence. A good brushing of the teeth is required. One thing you definitely need as an alcoholic is good self-discipline. You have to keep telling yourself, 'Don't overreact, don't act too much like a prat, and most definitely don't get too angry, and never violent for any reason because you haven't got good self-control.' Of course, a lot of twelve-year-olds get angry, but I had quite good self-discipline. Probably because if Frank and Dot *did* find out, well, let's put it this way; it wouldn't be, 'Come on now, son, let's sit down and have a chat.' I think you know what I mean. Also, as the years go on and you are becoming more and more a disciple of Lucifer, you are engaging more and more with people who will become close to you. How do you explain your constant aggression to them? You aren't going to say to them, 'Oh sorry, mate,' or 'Sorry, babe, but I've just drunk 2 litres of Frosty Jack.'

'Why not?' you may ask. Simple! Eight out of ten alcoholics don't want people to know what they are. I was one of these. I was a secret alcoholic. Not a few cans on the library steps for all the world to see. You may say I was a liar – I was, but only to myself. How you take this is your choice. I drank alone. Just me and my Friend. You may not believe this, but I had some self-respect and wasn't gonna sit down in a busy city scaring shoppers to death because I had a problem. I did drink in certain places in town, but always hidden. And this goes back to control. A lot of alcoholics haven't got it. I think in all the time of my drinking, me getting angry would have been witnessed no more than ten times. Oh, but believe me, loads more times I've been angry behind closed doors.

So now I'm twelve years old and I've got my own little bar going on some Tuesdays and Saturdays. I'm happy enough to do this from time to time, but always being one hundred and twenty per cent sure there would be no comeback on me. You may say, 'But you can't be certain.' Oh, believe me I was. I don't know what or why it is that at that age or just becoming a teenager, we are prone to take more risks. Kids will ride their bikes without hands on handlebars, some will try and climb the tallest tree, some will steal crisps and sweets from the shop they do their paperround from, which also happens to be the shop Frank goes to before he goes to work (yep, you guessed). What a beating I got for that! I even tried to insult my father's intelligence with one of the most pathetic get-me-off-the-hook excuses (lies) that you will ever hear. Anyway, if I thought that beating was bad, it would have been a mild one compared to the one I'd have got if Frank had found me taking the risks I began to take next.

Well, there were the very few days when not only was whisky at a low, but there wouldn't be a decent enough quota of the litre bottles of beer. But I still had the 1½-litre ones, so being at that age where you seem to take more risks, I started adding a little drop of them to my potion. As I have said, there were only five of these, but the amount you got out would compensate for the missing bottles. Say, for example, a 1½-litre bottle would make up for about two 1-litre bottles. 'Is that it?' you might say. Yeah, but I don't want to get caught, and don't want to appear smashed out of my head. The one problem with the 1½-litre bottles was that they could be a little bit excitable. By this I mean they could froth up a bit too much and would take longer to settle down than their younger brothers. Well, now I had my back-up resource if the litres were a bit lower than normal. I even started looking and seeing if there'd be enough litre bottles if I was planning the next day to invite my Friend round for a quick visit.

So, being a twelve-year-old, and having the need to take more risks, my brain was telling me, 'Come on, we need something more daring, more challenging. Come on, think, *think!* Aah, I know – got it! We are going to take the biggest gamble, biggest stomach-churning risk ever – never mind them sky divers or bungee jumpers, this will make them look like peas in a pod!' We've done the 1½-litre bottles of beer, now it's time to do the home-made wine. So we're going for the wine; then this would only be a Saturday dance with the Devil. Tuesdays were way too risky. Well, you may be thinking, 'What's the risk? Surely it's just a case of unscrewing the bottle, pour a bit out, replace with the water. A trained chimp could do that!' Oh, how I wish it were that simple. The trouble was, the wine bottles were *corked*. None of this put me off, however. Unscrew lid, pour, malarkey. This was very much a 'remembering how you've seen your father do it' exercise. Now I had seen Frank do this uncorking, re-corking exercise many a time, even helped him some.

Just let me explain how this procedure works. Firstly, equipment. Don't ask me the names of the tools I used, I wouldn't know. All of these were found in the kitchen, and some on the top of the wardrobe in my Dot and Frank's bedroom. Secondly, out to the shed to select our lucky winner. Here you had to be extremely careful. Some of them bad boys would fizz up so much, you'd lose quarter of a bottle, or even worse; it would explode. You had to check very carefully. OK, now we've selected the bottle with 666 on it, it's back to the kitchen. Now we unscrewed the lid (if only that was it) to reveal our nemesis: the cork. Grab the corkscrew from the drinks' cabinet, (it was one of those good ones with the handles) and proceed to unscrew the cork. Probably would take a little swig at this point, and add a little bit to our simmering cauldron. Now we've got all we need from bottle 666, it's time to re-close him. Thing is with re-closing the bottle, was when Frank done it, he had Dot to hold the bottle for him. I was a solo effort. Sounds easy in writing, but a little harder doing. Basically, you had to put the new cork in this wooden device – God knows the name – get it into the bottle hole, and pull the two arms down, thus sealing the bottle. Easy, yeah? No! Not at all easy. As I said, Frank had Dot to hold the bottle still; with me it was a case of putting the bottle between my feet, squeezing and praying as much as I could that my newly found chum wouldn't slip on the floor, emptying a lot of his fluids and leaving me sweating under the collar a bit every time a new bottle was to be opened by Frank at some occasion. You see, the wine wasn't an everyday tipple for Dot and Frank like the beer was. As it was, though, I never had to go through the perspiration bit with the wine and this opening and closing of the bottle was extremely rare. I may have wanted to take a risk or two, but I didn't have a death wish!

Well, I'm taking a few risks now. They seem to be getting a bit more daring. Definitely stupid, but hey, what the hell! People of my age take risks, so what can we do now for that buzz? Well, my mind was made up for me with that little word, *pressure*!

# CHAPTER
# Three

IN MY DAYS of being that young, innocent, angelic little cherub, I would play down this field with kids about four or five years older than me, and you know how it is; this little whippersnapper wants to show the big boys that he is also a big boy. When you're this tiny urchin, you want to show the big boys you can 'cut it with them', so these big 'chaps' who you idolise, treasure, worship the ground they walk on, whether they know it or not are manipulating you in their own way. So this is where we come to the word 'pressure'. Firstly they started trying to get me to smoke, which for a while I held out against, but then, being weak-willed, I succumbed to my heroes' pressure. Maybe the writing was on the wall then.

The next mission I was to embark upon concerning alcohol was pure suicide. Give me the gun and I'll put the gun against my head and pull the trigger myself! I'll always remember that evening down the field. Someone had got one of those large, vinegar-like containers – I think they're called flagons – full of Merrydown Cider from somewhere. Between them of us that were there – I can't recall how many there were – we delighted in emptying this container of its 'liquid death'. We were certainly merry. Satan had taken control of this young group of experimenters. We were swinging round the goalposts, stumbling into each other in a drunken show and generally larking about. Only with each other, though, not making a nuisance of ourselves to anyone else.

Now, during this episode, I spilled out that Frank made home-made beer and wine. Well, that was it, it became the task of the eldest scallywag, over the next couple of weeks, to pressurise me into taking a bottle of beer from Frank's cupboard and bring it down the field for everyone's enjoyment, although I don't really think I needed much pressurising. I was the youngest of our group and I wanted some status. Now the beer would have been enough to bring me status, but at that age, you want more. You want immunity, so now being this untouchable twelve-year-old, the mind is working overtime to get me immunity with the gang. So I'm thinking, 'What about *two* bottles of beer?' Nah, way too risky. One was risky enough, two would have been asking for capital punishment. 'How about I make one of my mixtures? No, not enough. Even I'm starting to get used to that. Ah! Got it! We'll go for a bottle of wine and take one of Frank's numerous bottle openers. Now we've got our objectives in mind, it's time to think of our master plan to complete our mission...'

With this daring venture, I always knew the beer was going to be the hardest item to get. Bottle opener; no problem, get that while Dot and Frank are enjoying their well-earned Sunday lie-in (already had that day in mind) – bottle of wine, easy! Grab that from the wine rack in the shed when I go to pick up my bike, and then shove it in my sports bag with, at the moment, just my football boots in (hoping to be accompanied by the beer and wine), so this part of the grand plan is easy. There is a bit of risk in all this, but nowhere near the risk of getting the beer. 'Why bother with the beer?' you may ask. 'You've got your wine, leave it at that; don't get greedy.' This is a very good question. My simple answer, again, is that I wanted immunity with the chaps. I wanted to be as near to being top dog as someone my age could be!

Well, the wine and corkscrew I had plans for; the beer had to be opportunist. The reason for this was that the beer was in the cabinet in the living room. Needless to say that the living room was pretty much occupied all the time by Dot, Frank or my brother, so I knew if the opportunity arose, it had to be wham bam thank you ma'am! You know what it's like at that age, your parents are talking to you, and you're nodding your head, muttering the occasional, 'Yeah.' But there was only one thing in my mind, as they're jabbering away. I'm just thinking, 'Shut up, and go out the room even if just for a couple of minutes' (wouldn't take me any longer).

Well, as the saying goes, seconds seemed like minutes, minutes like hours blah, blah, blah, and then we had our first movement. First to leave the soon-to-be 'crime' scene was my brother. He was only a little stumbling block in this. I knew when he went out, he'd be gone for a couple of hours. Now all we had to wait for was the 'big fish' to leave the room, for, as I said, just a couple of minutes. They had to be outside though. No way was I going to do it with them on the inside. Now Frank always sat in the chair next to the cabinet. I remember him going up to the toilet, so I decided to take up residence on his throne, thus getting me closer to my goal. Dot was still in the room and said something like, 'You'd better get out of Frank's chair before he gets down.' I thought, 'Why? I'm so close to my treasure.' So I stayed sat on his 'throne'. Don't know why; I mean, if he wasn't going outside, he'd just turf me out anyway, and as I said, I wouldn't be able to get my target with them in the house, but it just felt to me, the closer I was to my old mate, the easier it would be to release him from his prison cell and take him outside with me to have some fun. I persisted in staying in his chair up until he opened the living room door. Only then did I start to begrudgingly haul myself from the throne, only to hear sweet music to my ears as Frank said, 'It's all right, you can stay there. I'm going into the garden.'

Well, those few words certainly got the old pulse racing. That's one big fish out of the way, now my mind is thinking, *Please, please Dot, go out and join Frank.* I'm even starting to think up ideas to get her out there, but there was no need. Here are the words I've been waiting for: 'I'm going into the garden to give Frank a hand'. I just said a quiet, 'OK, Dot.' But in my head, the cheering, the celebration, the thought of, *Right, in a couple of minutes, this is it!*

Now they're both outside, I'm thinking fast, working fast. I know I have to hold it together; this is an absolute no cock-up operation. I slowly get up from the throne – not too quickly; if too fast, and one of my parents were to see me springing up like a jack in a box, their parent siren would go off, telling them, 'Son up to no good: check out'. Then it was a casual look out of the back window: the result was good, both of them down weeding. Now it's time to move fast, whip open my treasure chest: another look out of the window. Good, both still weeding. Grab my holy grail – any one will do. Another look out of the window. Great, still weeding! Close the treasure chest, a final look out of the window, still there (who says weeds are a nuisance?). Run up to my bedroom and put the beer in the bag with my football boots. There, smash and grab raid completed.

When it's time to go out, its a simple out the back door, in the shed to get my bike and, of course my crowning glory, the bottle of wine; a minute's ride down to the field to meet the chaps where I'll be the godfather, if only for one night. As we know with these ventures, they don't always run as smooth as a baby's bum. Mine was no different. I wasn't caught, but what happened to me when I was leaving for the field, still gives me a shudder now.

Well, it was only going to be about an hour's wait before I was off down to the field. I had mixed feelings; some feelings of nervousness, anxiety, just in case I was caught at the last hurdle, and, of course, feelings of excitement because if I pulled this off, I'd be the one being worshipped, and join the field folklore. This would be talked about for years. If it wasn't, you may as well have locked the door and thrown the key away.

Finally it's time. The time has now come to be a WINNER OR A LOSER. (Know which one I want to be.) So now it's up to my bedroom to collect my little swag bag. 'Ah, there's my baby, just waiting for Frankdy.' Plan: downstairs; out of door; wine; field! So I grab my bag and walk down the stairs. I'm just going out the backdoor and shout a goodbye to Dot and Frank. I'm there! I'm there! When all of a sudden, *Boom!* It felt like my heart was going to explode.

*Return Ticket Please*

Frank has called me back. Jesus Christ! Well, you know how people react in panic situations – well, I suppose everyone is different. My reaction was to get back through the kitchen and head back up to my bedroom, with Frank still calling me. When I was half way up the stairs, the calling went up a couple of decibels, so I just put my sack of 'gold' down on the stairs, and went downstairs to see what he wanted. And do you know what it was? Do you know why he almost gave his youngest son a heart attack? It was to say goodbye. The prat! If he wasn't Frank, and I wasn't doing wrong, I'd have punched him.

Well, now it's back to get the loot. That was easy enough. I just said, 'I'm going to the toilet, and then I'm off. Bye!' Now the old ticker's returning to normal, I grab my bag and toddle off into the shed to get my bike, and of course, the *crème de la crème*: the wine. It's there. I've done it! I've only gone and done it! The mission is completed with no casualties.

The excitement I had on getting to the field and revealing to the other chaps the treasure I had risked my life for, was extreme to say the least. So now here it was. No longer would I be looked on as the young one they took very little notice of. Now I had a bit of respect, which felt great, even if it did mean me almost losing my life. This is an absolute true story. Nothing here is fabricated in any way. Now it was time for me and the other lads to savour my catch. Never again did I attempt this – no way!

We've drunk, we've enjoyed. The others and me are on a high until I'm brought down to earth with a very minor bump by Dot. My time to be in during those kiddie years was 8.30 p.m., but on that night, as the power of Satan had taken over me, I was oblivious to the time. So when the eldest Camacho said to us all, 'Let's go to Dot's house,' we all followed like sheep. You see their 'be in by this time' lecture was a little different than mine, as they were older, but I went anyway. Why not, I was enjoying myself. I had stayed round there for about an hour over my curfew time, when I sensibly decided to make a move back home. I said my goodbyes to my light-headed comrades, and started on my way home. I hadn't even got out of my mates' field of vision when I saw Dot marching up the road to practically pull my arm out of its socket to march me home. I didn't care about the ear bashing I was getting, or the threats of 'Just you wait until Frank sees you' (which weren't actually threats). No, I was more concerned that this was all happening in view of the lads. How embarrassing. I mean – see it from my point of view. Here I am, twelve years old, I've undertaken an extremely risky mission which I've succeeded in, which has given me some status with the gang, only to have Dot drag me home like some little kid (which I was). Well, I can certainly tell you I wasn't looking forward to seeing the gang the next day, never mind what Frank was going to do to me.

I went down to meet up with the gang the next day, and was quite surprised that it was mentioned only the once. Someone said, 'Why did Dot come and get you last night then?' To which I pathetically answered, so as to keep status, 'Oh, she just came to say she might not be there when I got back because she was going up a friend's.' I don't know whether it was believed or not, but it wasn't questioned or mentioned again, so I presumed I had kept my newly acquired status.

Well, as I said I never attempted that again, but I still kept my own private bar going at home: the beer, whisky, occasional wine, but this was starting to get boring. Unfortunately, that was all that was available at my pub, except for about a month/month and a half of the year. That is when the big guns came in. Yep, you've guessed it! It was Christmas time.

Every Christmas time, as in most households, there were a variety of demons occupying the drinks cabinet. Wayhey! Of course there'd be our usual suspects; the beer, whisky and our bottles of wine outside in the shed. But at Christmas our regulars were joined by some new friends. This friendship may only last for about a month and a half, but whatever; all of us were to be acquainted in that short space of time. So, who were our new acquaintances? Well, we had vodka, gin, advocaat, sherry, port, Drambuie, Sheridan's, brandy and Bailey's. So as you can see there was quite an assortment to choose from. I said this new friendship probably only lasted about a month and a half, which it did. You may be thinking, A month and a half? Bloody hell that amount would last me a lifetime! But as I said, my parents were heavy drinkers, as in turn were their friends. Oh, but don't get me wrong; when I say the friendship would only last about a month and a half, well that is how long it would last for me. Yeah, by the middle to the end of January, we had reached the all too familiar territory of 'leave; way too risky'! So self-control prevailed and we bid our newly found friends a fond farewell in the knowledge that we would meet up again next year for our annual get-together. Now it was back to me and the old chums who, although being out of the limelight for that month and a half, never showed any resentment towards me.

So it's back to me and the old faithful. But that's OK; I'm only twelve years old and even though he's established himself inside me, he hasn't got total control of me yet. Even though these were lean spells, there were still opportunities for a brief reunion with the boys during the year. You see, Dot is a Scotswoman and when there was a special occasion, like a birthday or anniversary, she would do a slap-up meal, which meant that some – not all – of my mates from Christmas would pop back for a flying visit. Lucky bastards! They had four holidays a year: April, July, August and October were their times for visiting foreign climates and they had it cushty. No accommodation to pay for, a lovely warm and dry room to rest, and a very caring host.

# CHAPTER
# Four

SO, I'M TWELVE years old and I'm messing around with a very serious 'toy', but also doing the normal twelve-year-old things. I mean, there're fifty-two weeks in a year. I'm not doing this week-in, week-out; no, this is an occasional thing, when at that age you are not totally aware of what you are doing, and certainly not aware of the price you could pay in later life. So, as you're getting older, maturing, having different experiences, meeting new people, experiencing a whole load of different emotions, your brain is deciding what you do and don't like. In other words, the silent one. (By this I mean people can see the changes in your physical appearance – for example facial hair, genital hair, your voice breaking and so on, but they haven't got a clue what's happening inside the silent one and, to an extent, neither do you especially where alcohol is concerned; that understanding will come in later years or when it's too late.) So, as I'm going through my school life, enjoying the occasional tipple, I'm not an alcoholic – or am I? Is it my destiny? Could it be that as young as I am, there's no way out of it? I'm an alcoholic and every innocent drink is just food for the brain and if I tried – or even wanted – to stop, it wouldn't matter because you ain't going to beat the most powerful thing in the world; if it wants it, it gets it.

So here we have it. The Devil has viewed his new

accommodation; does he like it? Um... yes, he thinks he'll buy it but it's going to take a few years to get it to how he wants, so now let's get to work. So He begins his arduous task of making the perfect home.

I'm twelve years old; he has plenty of time. So now let's take a look at what He achieved.

Well, during my school and teenage years, my drinking habits followed the same pattern as when I was twelve, obviously, because I was still years away from being let into a pub/off-licence. So I was happy enough – didn't bother me, and then at sixteen we get the dreaded 'So what do you want to do when you leave school?' Now I wasn't a thick kid, but I wasn't a brain surgeon either. I didn't really have much of a clue of what I wanted to do, so I decided that I would apply for college to try and get on the catering course. Well, I'd been going one day a week in my final year at school, so it seemed the most sensible thing to do; plus 'cause I had been going for that one day a week, I was pretty much guaranteed a place on the two-year course. So there it was! Goodbye Highbury Secondary School, hello Salisbury College of Technology. I was now to begin my adolescent years, hoping to become a fully qualified chef. And as we know, catering and alcohol mix together pretty well. Yes, two years of training to hopefully become a fully qualified chef. Did you know that they say cheffing is one of the most high-risk jobs for becoming alcohol dependant? This obviously is down to the immense stress and pressure that the job involves.

Well, at sixteen, I wasn't getting involved in this high-risk career hoping that it would further my progress into becoming an alcoholic. No, I was stepping into this world of the unknown to halt the constant teacher and parent pressure that all sixteen-year-olds get. You know – 'You're almost an adult now, you're going to have to learn to stand on your own two feet.' So catering it was, and well, I can tell you what a shock to the system it was. I absolutely hated it. Who were these new people invading my life? Piss off! I don't know you and don't want to. This was all a thought in the head, of course; still got to have my self-discipline. It took me about a month to come to terms with college life, and this was because my Old Friend came out to play. I think, because my brain was in this state of confusion, it pressed the panic button and said to me, 'Do you remember them old days when a situation came up that you didn't like and we turned to Him? Well, why don't we do that again? Yeah why not! Bloody good idea!'

So there it was one morning – don't forget had to be a Tuesday. We made our old mixture, just the beer and whisky to start off with, and went to college with that light-headed, confident feeling of, 'Yeah I'm really looking forward to today,' and that's what it turned out to be; my best day at college yet and it was all down to Him. I mixed much more easily with the other students in my group. Yeah, so with His help, I had broken down barriers and from now on I would look forward to going to college, not with a drink inside me every day, but because He'd got me over that difficult hurdle, with a much more relaxed attitude. I was sixteen years old; I shouldn't have cared what these new people in my life thought of me, but I did; I was quite sensitive and He just made me forget my sensitivity and enjoy myself, so with this hurdle conquered, I wouldn't need my friend so much for now.

I would still see Him from time to time; I mean I had to, my brain demanded it, but at college you have the opportunities to go to college-organised discos or other special events that the catering department would organise, one of which was a very popular one. Yes, it was the good old Christmas piss-up. This was for catering students only and it involved us students having our Christmas dinner in one of the two college restaurants (the posh one) and having our dinner cooked and served by the lecturers and then boogying the night away at the disco organised for us. Unfortunately, my night was cut drastically short by the intervention of Him; yes, Him who was supposed to be my friend, barged in and gatecrashed my party. I recall me and a mate, Richard Paice, decided we would take a gamble and see if we could get served in Tesco's for some alcohol; you know what they say, if you don't try, you don't get. Well, our bravery was rewarded as we got served, no questions asked. Result! I think we got the cheapest bottle of white wine – yeah, a bottle of Hock. Well, that was it; we went back to Ritchie's mum's, swigged down our star prize, disposed carefully of our catch, and went to the party. So there were Rich and me at the party, eating, joking around and also being served more wine by the lecturers; red, white, rose, all of it going down my throat in no particular sequence. It could have been yellow with green spots on it, it was free, it was alcohol and I was there to enjoy myself.

There is always one major problem when you are that age and there is so much free booze floating around. You don't know how to limit or stop yourself from going way beyond the point of no return. I mean, you have to look big in front of the other students – you know the attitude: 'Aye, I'm sixteen, my name's Derek, look how big I am drinking all this booze. It's not affecting me.' But of course it is, and believe me, you don't half feel embarrassed and such a prat when you are being helped out of the disco throwing up and being led to the corridor to sit down for a breather with all the students gathering around you waiting for the next eruption from within you. God, don't you just wish the ground would open up and swallow you up? The main thing going through my mind at this time was why? Why me? And why don't the students just fuck off. This certainly wasn't in the script for that night, I can tell you. I mean, I'm Derek, I can handle my drink. What a total twat I was! Well, I don't remember how I got to the bench in the college reception, but that is where I was woken up by one of the lecturers asking how I was, did I feel up to going home? And so on, and so on. Amazing the sympathy you get when you are in that state. Ritchie, who was fine, was staying the night at Dot's. We left the college and, to my surprise, I was walking quite well, considering how I was at the college party. I got a good night's sleep, and incredibly woke up the next morning feeling OK. Dot and Frank found the whole episode very funny. Dot cooked me and Ritchie a full English which I wolfed down, no problem. There was none of this, 'Aargh! I can't face this crap.' Well, you'd never have thought I would be so fresh, considering the night before, or was I just still light-headed? Whatever it was, I didn't want to be in the state I was in the night before, so I told myself, as so many of us do when we've been drunk for the first time, 'That's it, I'm not drinking ever again.'

Well, I got the expected mickey-taking at college the next day. Gone was the sympathy of the night before. Now it was the turn of the arseholes who had never experienced the state I was in the night before. Not to worry though, I just shrugged my shoulders and said, 'Yeah, funny. I've heard all you've got to do is open a bottle and you're pissed.' Not a great response, but it was all I could think of at the time, and anyway, I wasn't going to show these dipsticks that my blood was boiling on the inside. As I said, Ritchie was fine that night. *Why?* Well I s'pose I must have just drunk more than him. I mean we had the bottle of wine beforehand; I presumed we'd had the same, or was it that I was taking bigger gulps than him? Or was it that during the meal I was getting my wine glass topped up more frequently than he was, because I thought I could handle it, and also wanted to look big? Was it that? Although I had sampled Frank's homemade wine on numerous occasions, that wine was just not my drink. You know what I mean; you're always hearing people saying, 'Oh yeah, I can drink twenty pints of lager in a session and it doesn't affect me, but give me a short, phew, then I'm pissed.' But no, I think we'll just put it down to an excited, immature sixteen-year-old trying to look big.

Well I was very lucky that the day after the party was our last day before the Christmas holidays, so I didn't have to endure much piss taking. Just a couple of days after my fall from grace, it was time for 'the season to be jolly'. Yes, the time of the year when all of my mates would gather round for one of their seasonal holidays; only problem was that this holiday I had told myself that I wasn't joining in with them. Would I stick to my threats?

Well, they do say that Christmas is the time to be jolly and my threats meant nothing. Christmas Day dinner when offered a glass of wine, I thought it would be rude to refuse; how weak-willed is that? Once again, He'd got to me. As always, my brother refused. I thought to myself, *He doesn't know what he's missing out on*, but now I know he wasn't missing out on anything. How I wish I'd been more like him.

Even though I'd fallen to His powers again, I wasn't sitting at the dinner table going to myself, 'Oh please, I must have some, give me some.' Not at all, but in my subconscious, He was creeping in bit by bit, inch by inch. I'm one hundred per cent certain of that. I mean, I knew that other of my mates were relaxing in Dot and Frank's bedroom, and, just occasionally, he'd give me a little reminder of this, so on some visits to the toilet I'd quickly nip into Dot and Frank's bedroom to check up on my mates. I'll tell you what his powers are: overpowering. Anyway, I think He must be pretty pleased with Himself. He's looked after me from childhood and into my adolescence. He was my guardian and I was His servant. Now he's got me, can He keep hold of me, as I start my second year of college?

Well, here I am, beginning my second year of college. I am now seventeen years old. At the moment I am under the beginnings of a very evil spell. I say beginnings because He hasn't got the total control that He wants over me yet. Maybe He saw me as a special case and wanted to take His time and get this one absolutely right. Believe me, flattered I'm not.

Anyway, the second year at college meant that us wannabe

chefs/waiters were let loose into the college's main restaurant. Yes, this was the restaurant where we were let loose to cook and serve the brave public (no – we weren't *that* bad). The restaurant seated about thirty-five covers and the public got a very good priced meal; a three-course meal was about £3.75 and a four-course was about £4.75, so a very good deal. Now the idea of the restaurant wasn't just for us students to get the food from the kitchen and slam the plate down in front of the customer and say, 'Enjoy your meal.' No, we were a silver-service restaurant. Each of us would be allocated our area of the restaurant by the headwaiter, who had also done the table plan. By the way, this headwaiter was a student not a lecturer. Now with every table covered (it was always full), the headwaiter would tell the other students what their job was to be that session; a restaurant just doesn't operate on customers being fed.

The college was very proud of this restaurant. It was called The Wessex Restaurant and was run to the standard of a three-star hotel, so every aspect of it had to be covered by us students. So what other jobs do we have apart from serving food? Well, we have the cashier (pain in the ass). This poor person had to take the customers' money, and at the end of service, do the cashing up. Well this is where the pain in the ass bit came. Nearly every service, the cash never tallied up properly, meaning that the poor sod who was cashier would be trying to get the totals to match while all the other students were at lunch. Once done, you got your lunch but it wasn't half a lonely one. I tried to get out of the cashier's job as much as possible and did. Think I only done it no more than four times. Anyway, why would I want to be cashier when there were much more eye-catching positions in the restaurant to be had, such as wine waiter or barman? Oh yes, the demonic thoughts would brainwash me if I was selected to do one of those jobs and believe me; I had my fair share of brainwashing over the year. All the wine waiter's job involved was showing the wine list to the customer (hoping they would choose a bottle or carafe), opening the bottle at the table (bit nerve-racking), giving the host first taste to make sure it's pukka, then whizzing round the other customers. Of course this left just over a quarter of the bottle; now it was a waiting game (pardon, no pun intended). You see, some customers would finish the whole bottle (fair dos – they paid for it), but some would leave a gulp in the bottle. Wayhey! This is where I'd come in. Yep, gulp of wine, me, Him; there's only one outcome. Not out in the restaurant, but a quick nip into the bar wash-up area, where instead of being disposed of down the sink, it was disposed of down my throat (thank you). Well, that was the perk of being the wine waiter. The perks of being barman were even better! All the barman's job involved was getting the drinks order from the waiter and doing them up: for example a half a bitter, gin and tonic, vodka and tonic and a glass of house wine. Well now, it felt like you were in heaven, all them different drinks we had to choose from. I say 'we' because we were all doing it (I wonder how my fellow students turned out?) I mean, we were never totally pissed out of our heads, just happier I s'pose. I never did this every waiting session, but it was more an indication of Him gaining control of me.

# CHAPTER
## Five

WELL, AFTER getting over the first few weeks of college, I loved it, and the things and drinking I was doing were surely just natural for a seventeen-year-old student? Believe me, there were numerous occasions to exploit my new found love; yep, there were discos, parties, days out and trips abroad. One of these trips was to France for five days and I was going on it.

Yeah, the trip to France was supposed to be educational, but this was a group of seventeen/eighteen-year-old college students. Get real! There was only one thing on my and probably ninety-five per cent of the other students' minds and that was to get boozed up. And why not? For the first time for the majority of us, we were away from our parents – yeah away from all them rules and regulations we had at home. Yeah, sure, we had the lecturers, but they were pretty laidback.

So the drinking begins on the ferry over – nothing over the top, just a couple of pints. After all, we were students, not a pack load of England supporters going to wage war on the opposition, and anyway, I think more than a couple would have resulted in the English Channel taking on a different shade. Our destination in France was Paris, but unbeknown to us – don't know whether the lecturers knew – we were staying in the red light district. Yep, we're talking

*Return Ticket Please*

Moulin Rouge country. It was certainly a shock for students and lecturers, but whatever; us students just wanted to drop our luggage off and explore, which is what we did.

Well, the amount of prostitutes, drug pushers and sex shops was incredible and was certainly an eye-opener for us students. We did ask how much it was to go into the Moulin Rouge but it was £52; way above our limit, and anyway we were there for booze, not some sexed-up cabaret. As you probably know, it is far easier to get served alcohol in France than our country as their lawful age for being able to drink is seventeen and – well, didn't we take advantage of that, especially on the first night. I don't think there was one of us not pissed. God we were loud, especially one of my best mates Jason Grey. I've known Jay for twenty-eight years and because of his falling down stairs, shouting and swearing, we were almost chucked out until the lecturers put a stop to it and convinced the owners it was just overexcitement (bless Jay).

Well, our trip went with no more mishaps and it was time to get back to good old Blighty via, of course, the duty-free. Funnily enough I didn't get much duty free; nah I just got forty-eight bottles of them 50 ml bottles of lager. Never mind, they were enough for a bit, plus I still had Frank's home-made beer, wine and the whisky.

Well, my two years at college had come to an end, and I'd passed my first- and second-year exams. Yeah, I'm a qualified chef. There are loads more stories from college, but this book is about my losing battle with the Devil, not my life story.

While at college, I took on a part-time job at an Italian

restaurant in the city centre. This restaurant would have been heaven for any alcoholic and was soon to become for me. It was called Don Giovanni's. So here I am, a fresh-faced, innocent (ha!) seventeen-year-old, working Friday and Saturday nights from five thirty to midnight, and I'll tell you what it was that so different from college. If you don't learn to adapt to it fast, woah, you're in big trouble. This is the time in your life when, if you're smart, you'll learn to keep your mouth shut and that you don't know everything. Yeah, each job is different, but at Don G's, you'd better button it or have some mad Italian chef after you with a meat cleaver and that's the truth. Bit of a shame there aren't a few more places around like that today. Might teach these know-it-all teenagers some manners and a bit of respect for people who've done a little bit more than them. We live in hope…

Anyway, let's get back on track with the book. So here I am, I'm seventeen years old and *Boom!* I've been chucked into this new world. I'm like a lost little boy. I'm nervous, scared, won't say boo to a goose. Well, I suppose that's to be expected. At DG's, most of the staff is foreign. In my seven odd years there I worked with Italian, French, Spanish, Moroccan, Zimbabwean, Portuguese, Turkish, German, Irish and Scottish people. Yeah, I think that's about it. The thing about working with these older, more experienced foreigners was that I didn't half get embarrassed a lot… Oops, sorry, I'm deviating again. Let's cut to the chase. You know what made DG's really great? Well, it was the fact that you could drink there. Now I don't mean you could bring in a couple of cans of your own; no, our very generous boss – a certain Alf Bowley – let us have whatever we wanted from behind the restaurant bar. Well, not exactly; we couldn't have spirits – not that he knew of – but we could have lager or bitter, and it was unlimited. There was one bloke there called Angus who would have about ten or more pints of bitter a day. Now with this prime opportunity, you'd think I'd be guzzling down relentlessly; but no, I wasn't at first. Like I've said, He was inside me, but He didn't have total control – yet. No, believe it or not, I was quite happy to have the occasional pint or two, nothing more; but eventually I would go into uncharted territory.

You see, I was a young pup, very quiet, might mumble about fifteen words a night, but then one New Year's Eve night, the beast inside me ordered me to have more. You know, let your hair down a bit. So I obeyed His command. I must have had about five pints of lager that night and the results were great. I think in that one night I spoke more than the whole time I'd been there, and once again, it was all down to Him. But what would happen next? I mean the next time at work – would I be that laugh a minute character we'd seen on New Year's Eve? Or would I be that timid little boy who we'd seen so much over the past?

Well, as it was, He'd broken the ice for me but I wasn't a five pint a night person yet, which meant He had to work a bit harder on me. As I got moved up from starter chef to pizza chef, that little word came in again. Yep: pressure. But not the kind of pressure I had had from the older kids; no, now it was work pressure. Yep, going from starter chef to pizza chef was a shock to the system. Way more pressure and yeah, I made mistakes, but the difference from these and college mistakes was a bit more scary. So to combat the mad Italian chef's bollockings I'd have a pint, and do you know what? It would work wonders, to the extent that I would perform better. Now this wasn't every time I worked as pizza chef – oh no! Once I'd got over that initial hurdle, it would be occasionally, so He still had more work to do. My boss helped Him out a little bit with His busy workload. Oh yes! Our boss had sacked the head chef, and who should spring to his mind as the new head chef? Me! Yeah, it meant another £50 a week in my wage packet, but it also meant a load more pressure. So who'd pop straight into my mind to get me over that hurdle? Yep: Him.

As I got older and more and more challenges were being put in front of me, the more He was appearing in my life. Whilst pizza chef, I'd got into the habit of going to the pub between lunch and dinner service. Now this was a three-hour interval where me and a couple of mates would play darts, pool and pinball, and, of course, drink; this is where He first introduced me to the real Devil's drink; yeah, cider. At first it was the Strongbow, but then He stepped up the pace and saw if I could keep up with it and He introduced me to the real Devil's drink; yeah, Diamond White. What a killer of a drink that is. I'd have two or three in my three-hour break from work and go back feeling more relaxed and confident (great feeling) and at DG's when that feeling was leaving me, it was just a case of asking a waiter/ress for another pint. I'm about twenty now. I'm not stupid, am I? So why am I following this path of self-destruction? God knows. You see, I was only a mortal and I was trying to fight off an immortal. There was only ever going to be one winner; Him.

So now His grip is getting stronger and stronger. He

orders me to take another risk, and I s'pose this one could have cost me my job if caught. This one wasn't as risky as taking Frank's home-brew, but there was still an element of risk. You see, as well as the free lager that was coming my way, I was also taking gulps of the white and red cooking wine and the cooking brandy. I'm not joking, but it was like them Christmases I had when younger; you know, the ones where all my friends would come round for a month or so, but now it was beginning to happen more frequently. Looking back on it now, God knows how I didn't see it spiralling out of control. Not once did I think to myself, *Come on Derek; get a grip, you're an alcoholic.* No, not once. He had brainwashed me, but then I had a stroke (no pun intended) of luck.

A stroke of luck, yeah; you see, with all the booze and food I was consuming I ballooned up to sixteen stone. Wow! Sixteen stone! Believe me, I didn't like that, so it was time for a strict diet and this diet didn't include Him. The temptation that He threw in front of me was unbelievable for the two months I was dieting, but somehow I resisted Him. I tell you what though, it wasn't half boring without Him, and it was like my right arm had been cut off. You see, the thing is, without Him I was a totally different person. I was quieter, didn't laugh so much and wasn't really interested in anything going on around me. God, I needed Him. The thing I hated most about not having Him around was when people would go, 'You're quiet, Derek, you OK?'

'Yeah I'm fine,' I would say; it's all you can say, isn't it? Can't exactly say, 'No I'm bloody not I ain't got my Friend with me,' can you? That's number one rule for a heavy drinker or alcoholic; you try to make everyone else think you hardly drink at all. Well, you do if you're a secret drinker.

Well, now I've got down to a weight I'm happy with, it's time to get reacquainted with my old Friend. Now we're back together, I don't want Him to go again, so I'll simply cut down my food intake, which is what I did. Now I'm drinking at work, on my break from work, on my days off, I'm even nipping into the offy to get a couple of cans to have while walking to Dot's. (Drunk in secret.) Now I'm starting to get cans in the afternoon so as to have to drink in the morning before I go to work. I've even got the keys for the restaurant now, so on a Sunday I'm getting there before everyone else so that I can have a couple of pints before the other staff arrived. Me and a couple of waiters are mixing the spirits to try and create the perfect cocktail. Occasionally after night time service, three or four of us would hang on drinking the free beer until the cockerel crowed. Up in the nightclub, the manager would ask, 'What do you want then, mate, top shelf?'

'Yeah, go on then.' All free of charge. I often wonder if this hadn't been my first job with so much free booze, would I have turned out different? That we will never know, but one thing's for sure: at this time of my life, not only had He planted His seed, but also His seed was growing inside me fast.

Well, I walked out of DG's after an incident occurred, so I was jobless but certainly not penniless. Oh no! Over the years of good pay and cheap rent, I had accumulated something in the region of four grand, so I may not have been getting any more free booze, but I certainly had enough to keep my hunger fed, and that's what it was now; a hunger, not a pleasure. When I had all that money, He seemed to be the only thing on my mind. I mean, it didn't matter that I had no money (apart from the Dole) coming in, just as long as me and Him were having fun, and anyway if my money was getting low, He'd help me out just like He always did, wouldn't He?

Well, as my money was dwindling, it was then that I thought I might have a bit of a problem. Now you might think to yourself, 'You thought you might have a bit of a problem?' Well yeah, you see, as an alcoholic you never have a problem with drink but everyone else has. Oh yeah, everyone else is the alcoholic, not you.

The definite clinching point was when, with my ex-wife, I had £1 left in my pocket. Yep, just one measly pound. Well, of course, that went on a can of super-strength cider. I walked a couple of miles to somewhere up Bemerton Heath to drink my last can. It was a sad moment, a bloody sad moment. I was gone for hours and my ex was pulling her hair out with worry. In all this time, I did a lot of thinking and decided I had to tell my ex about my Friend. He tried to dissuade me but no, I had to. When I got home I was greeted with genuine concern. How could I say anything now? I'd never cried out for help before, so why start now? To mine and His shock, surprise, and delight, my ex and me sat down with me ready to spill my guts and she opened a bottle of advocaat. Well, I was feeling extremely nervous about telling her, so as He was screaming to me, 'You need me, you can't do this without me!' I accepted a glass. I think it was about four glasses later that He gave me the permission to tell her. 'But be warned: this won't mean you won't see me again.' How right He was.

Well, I explained to my ex-wife that I thought I had a drinking problem. Not an alcoholic, because I couldn't accept that myself yet; no, just a drinking problem. She listened and definitely didn't have a clue where I was coming from. I s'pose it's hard to understand something like that if you ain't been there. Well, whatever. She did start making sure I had no money each day to acquire drink, and I must admit that after the first few torturous weeks, I was getting used to not having Him around. No, that's not strictly true; I would still see Him in moderation and always with my ex-wife, so He was still there inside me. His flame might not be burning brightly, but burning it was.

So after weeks of this moderation, my sneaky side woke up. Yeah, He was getting used to His quota of food; He wanted more, and if He wanted more I had got to get Him more. Now enter the sneaky side. Every payday I'd sneak a couple of quid and put it inside my socks. This would be used on Mondays after I had walked my ex to work. Well, that was one day taken care of, what about the rest? Weekends were all right because after giving my ex her money, I'd do a little shop with the rest. This little shop, of course, included the cheapest and strongest cider I could get. Now my ex didn't mind this because it was for social drinking with her; she didn't mind and He certainly didn't. But as time passed, the body was getting used to Him. So now I've got to think of something else to satisfy His craving. Well there was only one solution I could think of. I'd have to ask my ex for some money at lunchtime so I could get some food. Only thing was, she wasn't thinking about the same food as me and I wasn't getting Him at lunchtime, but after I finished work. But what happened next was amazing. I confessed to my ex what I was really doing with the money, and do you know what? She kept giving it to me. Unbelievable! There I was thinking He'd be out of my life, but no; she was encouraging Him! Well, I wasn't going to argue and neither was He.

Now He was growing stronger and coming in the form of a litre bottle of Frosty Jack's. He had an immense stranglehold over me; I'd left my ex twice because I got some money and only Him and me were going to enjoy it. Thing is, when the money went I had no one to play with, so I'd have to go back to the ex. God knows why she took me back, it was only Him that made me get married, Him that made me walk out them times; basically, He was making a lot of decisions for me, and looking back now, a lot of wrong ones. It was one step telling my ex-wife (not that it helped much) but now it was time for the ultimate challenge; yep, it was time to tell the parents.

I had to tell them, they're my parents. They had every right to know that their little boy was in trouble. Yeah, I may have been twenty-two and an adult in the country's eyes, but in my little world I was a lost little boy and I was getting more and more seriously lost. I didn't know what the outcome of this bombshell to my parents would be. I think I was hoping for some magic cure. You know the sort of thing: 'My parents know now, I'll be fine, I'm cured.' Ha! Fat chance. Well, I knew that I wouldn't be able to tell them on my own so I had to visit Him for moral support, a bit of encouragement. I was surprised at how happy He was to help me – yeah, help me, bollocks! He was still inside me, still with me; He was like a shadow, He wouldn't fucking leave me alone.

I asked Dot and Frank to sit down; there was something I had to tell them. I will admit, He was making this a lot easier for me. Well anyway, I told them everything, and I think for the only time ever, (that's then and now) my whole emotional feelings came out. God, did they ever! I cried, cried, cried, cried and cried some more. Dot joined in a bit, Frank never did. He is so laidback he's horizontal. Frank said that when he was younger, he had been going down that same path but then met Dot so that stopped him. 'Yeah,' He probably thought, 'I've missed one Williams I'll get his son.'

Anyway, when all the crying had stopped, we talked about why I was like this and of course what I was going to do about it (well, us). Dot said she'd come to AA with me but I refused to go. I said, 'My problem, I'll deal with it.' Anyway, I'm not like them people at AA; they're old winos, drunks with no shame. Only thing is, I *was* like them people, but I refused to see it. Anyway, I was going to do this alone. Please. Dot and Frank asked how much I'd drunk today. I told them. I even said to them that I was looking at Frank's drinks cabinet and the one inside me was practically ordering me to get a drink. Well, we finished our talk with me saying to Dot and Frank that I just knew when I was walking home I'd go into the Spar for a litre bottle of cider. Dot tried her best to dissuade me and even though I said to her, 'OK, Dot, I won't.' Him and me knew otherwise. He'd even got the power to make me ignore Dot. Woah! Now that's some power.

I think the worst thing about telling someone you are an alcoholic is that instantly you think they're going to disown you, that they'll think of you as a lowlife; well, they don't. It's when you tell someone close to you that you are one that it should click inside you that you are cared for and if you need help it's there. In my case it didn't. He had me just where He wanted me and was enjoying His time with me. When I went to see Dot on my weekly visit, I had Him inside me and was covering His fumes with extra strong mints, as Dot would ask me how I was doing with the drink, to which I answered most of the time, 'Yeah OK. It's getting easier.'

Well now, with the closest people in my life knowing my situation and what I'd become, you'd think it would be easy to rid myself of Him – not a chance! He wasn't leaving – well, not permanently. He'd leave for short breaks, not leave but just wouldn't visit as frequently. One of these occasions was when my ex and me moved to Dorchester.

We did a house swap and on the day of the move He took it upon Himself to offer another pair of hands – yep, you see another stressful time in my life and He was there to cradle me through it (aah, bless Him) so the move went as sweet as it could – well, it did in my mind, but then my mind was His mind, wasn't it? I don't know why, but in Dorchester, I managed to keep Him at bay more than before. I think, in a way, this was a golden opportunity to exorcise Him from my body and brain. It was time for me to gather up all my strength and show Him what I was capable of and it did work for a bit. He would maybe not be seen for a week, which may not sound long, but for an alcoholic to go a week without a drink is like a rabbit having his dick cut off.

Now, was it really my own inner strength fighting Him off or was He just dormant? Whichever it was, my time in Dorchester was spent largely without Him. Except for one week, but before this one week I never drank before or after work, and me and my ex-wife only went to a pub about four times during my stay down there. I would still see Him on the occasional weekend, but only in a very small dose. Had I beaten Him? Driven Him out of me? Ha! Don't make me laugh, because when my ex and I mutually decided on a divorce, that was it. He came rushing back to me. My last week in Dorchester was spent at a workmate's place and I had my own money. (Trouble ahead.) Yep, every day after work I'd pick Him up from Asda and we'd head to the green and He'd delight in the fact that He was back with me. He'd ram it into me that I didn't have the power to discard Him. He'd say, 'You ain't got the will to lose me for ever!' He was right. I mean, any kind of problem that cropped up in my life and it was Him I'd run to, wasn't it? Well, I was moving back to my parents now; maybe there I could find the magic spell to get rid of Him totally. What the hell was I dreaming about? I mean, He was even on the bus from Dorchester to Salisbury with me. A quick nip into the offy, and He's walking to Dot's with me. Bloody hell! He's like a bodyguard. Well, now we're back. I get the question's asking if I'm slowing down my drinking. 'Yes, of course,' was the answer every time. Don't know why I didn't just ask for help; I suppose, in a quirky sort of way, I was too stubborn, too proud. Yeah right! Too ashamed, more like. Whatever it was, I wouldn't have any choice but to banish Him from me if I didn't get a job soon, as my last month's pay from my job in Dorchester was running out and I certainly wouldn't be able to keep Him happy with measly Dole money.

So any job was going to do me: bin man, kitchen porter, cleaner; even a toilet cleaner for the council would do. As it was I got a job for Avonmore dairies as a milk loader, which basically involved the transfer of milk cartons from the cavalbelt to the trolleys. Jesus Christ, was this the most boring job ever or what? But He would say to me, 'Come on, it's a job, which means there's money in, which means we can stay together.' (Christ, were we married?) He was right though, wasn't He? I mean, for our relationship to continue, I needed money. Although the job was brain-dead boring, it did have its perks. It was well paid for such a tedious job and you were paid weekly (cool).

At Avonmore I didn't really mix with many people, solely down to the fact that I wasn't using His services for a while. Why I don't know. I mean, it wasn't a conscious effort because don't forget I wasn't an alcoholic. (Right!) Anyway, just in case any of you were worried, don't be. I mean, He was still with me on days off. Big style and true to form, He started sneaking back into my working life, as I started to have cans before going to work. Workmates would comment, saying, 'Have you been drinking?' I'd answer, 'Yeah, had a quick pint before coming to work.' It wasn't a shock to any workmates because the majority were doing the same or smoking a joint.

As you can see, it wasn't a difficult job. I never drank while working there (God, wish I had), but started to after finishing. 'So what?' you might say. Well, the thing was that we'd alternate morning and night shifts. Obviously it was no problem getting any booze after the morning shift, as we finished at 3 p.m., but the night shift was a bit different. On the night shift there was no set time to finish; you finished when all the work was done, which meant a lot of the time we'd finish after closing time at pubs and off-licences. Well, in this predicament I had only one choice, which was to get Him before work and take Him with me. I'd stuff Him in my bag, shove the bag in our changing room and cover it with my clothes, praying that nobody found Him. Not because I was afraid of getting the sack, but because they would probably have drunk Him. So anyway, when I finished work I'd walk with Him to Elizabeth Gardens and release the Prince of Darkness out into His world.

With Him inside me, the long walks home became much more bearable. I'd sit down with Him in the gardens and have some fascinating conversations, just Him and me. It was so peaceful, man to immortal. Despite the amount of alcohol I was drinking at this point of my life, I never said, or thought I'd ever say, I was an alcoholic to anyone, apart from the people who I'd already told. God no! People have their own problems, which are far more serious than my drinking too much. That is how I saw it. I was just a heavy drinker; I was no different than Frank or half the people I knew, but of course I was. Where these people would suffer a terrible hangover and go through the day feeling like shit, I would just ask Him for a little chat and He'd oblige. At this point in my life, I'd forgotten what a hangover was. It was around this time that I was getting the first signs of needing Him. Yeah, just the first signs. It wasn't boom, just overnight I needed Him. He was still breaking me down but His powers of persuasion were by far outdoing my powers of resistance. My days off were spent totally with Him, some moments on our own, and some with a group of mates. It didn't matter to either of us what the situation was, just as long as we were together. There are so many stories of Him and me that I have in my brain, so many memories with Him; some good, some bad, some funny and some sad. I couldn't possibly write them all down in this book, these will be written in my next book…

# CHAPTER
## Six

WELL, HERE I was in the early stages of needing Him and in a boring job. Something had to change; it certainly wasn't going to be Him, was it? He wouldn't allow it, so a new job it was then. Well, I got a job back in catering thanks to His assistance at the interview. Looking back on it now, I needed Him but back then it was a case of Him just being there.

The journey to this new job was a nightmare. I had to travel about six miles but I don't drive, so I'd get the bus into town, walk to Dot's to pick up my brother's bike and cycle the remaining four miles (nightmare). I wasn't going to do this alone, so each day before work, I'd buy a cheap litre bottle of Him (Frosty Jack) and consume Him at different stages of my journey to Dot's, where sometimes I'd have a gulp of His harder brother, whisky. It was the same procedure on the way home, minus the whisky. I'd walk home and stand for hours in a peaceful, secluded area, just Him and me. I'd think about my past and the things that had gone wrong; things that should've happened but didn't; people who'd let me down and why. In my mind, there was only one person not letting me down and that was Him, but in reality it was Him letting me down, wasn't it? I was at my happiest just standing there with Him. My only concern was that of making sure I remembered to pick Him up from the shop for the next day's adventure.

*Return Ticket Please*

I started to play football for Porton FC on Sunday mornings, and even then I'd drink a 3- or 4-litre bottle of vodka I'd bought the day before. I'd drink this on my way to Dot's where I'd get picked up and play ninety minutes pissed out of my head. Nobody knew I was pissed because of my good self-discipline. I'd play better with Him inside me, I'd work better with Him inside me; anything I did seemed like it was much better with Him inside me. Or was that just a load of crap? Who knows? I mean, without Him could I have achieved what I had in my life so far, or without Him could I have achieved so much more? You decide. Whichever one, it didn't or doesn't matter now.

Another time when I drank Him openly and didn't think anyone would think I had a problem was on a week's holiday to Ibiza. Jesus Christ, that was morning, noon and night. Yeah, not just me though. God knows how many new friends I made on that holiday. I couldn't possibly remember them all. It was a great holiday though!

Well, I went back to the same routine of Him, work; work, Him, and He started to show me a side of Him I'd never seen. You see, in all of my working life I'd probably had about five days off sick and they were all legit, but now He was ordering me on some days to forget about work. 'Just leave it, spend the day with me, just go back to bed and when you wake up we can spend a nice relaxing day together.' So I'd obey. I probably had more days off in two months than I did in my whole working life. With this happening, I decided it was time for another job. He agreed, so my notice was handed in and I started work in another Italian restaurant called La Gondola as a kitchen porter, a job in which from two thirty to five I was entirely on my own in the restaurant to clean. Unfortunately for me, the bar was always locked when the chefs and waiters had left.

'Never mind,' He'd say, 'I've got an idea and it's simple…' And simple it was. All He told me to do was to empty a normal sized bottle of mineral water and then just fill it up with Him, pop Him inside my coat pocket and wait for all the staff to leave and just sit down with Him and talk, think and wait for five to come and stock up again for that night and next day. The stock was getting a bit more now, my body, brain, He was now demanding about three litres of the strong stuff plus what I'd drink sociably, which was God knows how much. I gave this job up as well, partly because of Him and partly because I was going to Australia for a month. Yep, good old Oz for a month and this was going to be *my* holiday and not His, well not so much of a holiday for Him as He'd expect, and so it was. For one month He was only seen on a much lower scale than He'd have liked. So why could I keep Him at bay in this holiday situation? I mean, one of the things you look forward to on holiday is consuming more alcohol than you would normally, isn't it? Well, it is for most people, but you see in my case this was a totally different experience. There were people I didn't know and vice versa. The difference between these people and the new people I'd meet in a new job, where I'd need Him to aid me through that getting-to-know-you period, was that the people I'd see and talk to on holiday I'd never see again so I could be a total prat and it wouldn't matter.

Well, after the month was up, He stormed back into my life and I didn't resist. He'd been away for a month and that was far too long for both of us, so I went back to the routine of stashing Him in my wardrobe and nipping up to my room for a few glugs whenever He needed me. The lads who I was living with surely must have suspected something at my constant going up and down stairs, but if they did what would they have said? Which one would have been brave enough to confront me on my strange behaviour?

Around this time, I did tell someone else. She enjoyed three or four glasses of wine a day herself. When I told her, the response I got was one of, 'Don't be stupid, you're not an alcoholic, you're over exaggerating.' Excuse me, but I think that I'm the one who knows whether I'm an alcoholic or not. So there we had it, another person who couldn't or wouldn't accept my problem. I was starting to accept it, so why were the people who knew sweeping it under the carpet? I needed help, but I was obviously not shouting loud enough. But then again, there's a massive difference between *needing* and *wanting* help. His spell was still upon me, and one day He decided to show me a little example of His awesome power. The fact that I never learned from this experience proves the persistency of the Devil.

Yeah, one fateful day that should have given me the will power to exorcise this evil inside me. At this stage of my addiction money was running out fast, but that was not deterring me or making me slow down with Him. No, if anything, it was getting faster. You see, He had stripped me of all my rational thinking. Without a regular wage coming in, I was picking up any sort of cash-in-hand jobs from mates. One of these was clearing a warehouse of computers in Birmingham; easy work for £150. The thing was though, I made one fatal mistake; I only had enough of Him inside me for three-quarters of the day. I didn't take Him with me; I only drank about two litres of Him before we left for Birmingham. Boy was he not happy about that. You see, for weeks prior to this job I had had anxiety feelings. I knew they had something to do with Him. I think there wasn't enough of Him inside me so He'd call to me and I'd top myself up with Him and He'd make me feel better, so once again there I was thinking He was my cure when in fact He was my parasite. What a major mistake, then, going to Birmingham and not taking Him with me. He was really pissed off and showed it. When half way back from Birmingham He was starting to show me how pissed off He was, yeah, the anxiety feelings started to come and He wasn't with me.

I was praying we'd get to Fordinbridge soon; this was where we were going to drop the computers off. I was yawning, trying to sleep, singing tunes in my head; anything to take my mind away from the anxiety He was inflicting on me. Nothing worked; the panic inside me was reaching a critical point. We eventually got to Fordinbridge with me in a right state. I'll tell you what, I needed Him at this stage to rescue me. Funny that, craving for the force that has inflicted this demonic spell on me, but there was no chance of getting Him anywhere (too late) so for the first time since I'd met Him, I was on my own, and believe me, it was the most frightened I'd ever been in my life. Well, He'd certainly taken over me at this stage but why? Why all of a sudden put me through this? Why? I mean, I thought I'd been a good disciple. I'd done everything He'd asked of me, hadn't I?

Why? Huh I'll tell you why, because He is just pure fucking evil, that's the reason why. It's as simple as that.

Well, my anxiety had reached such a level that I thought I was going to die and that's no bullshit. I was screaming at my mate, 'This is it, this is it! Do something!' They sat me down and that was it, the next thing I remember was gaining my senses and being in hospital. Hospital, yeah. Some bloody mate He was, putting me there! The doctor came round and asked me questions; you know the normal medical stuff (blah, blah, blah) and of course how much of Him I drank a week. Well, I think that unless you're a teetotaller, everybody lies in answer to this question and I was no different. Weird really; despite what He'd put me through, I was still prepared to lie on His behalf. What a stupid idiot I was because when they were going to let me out of hospital, He struck again. *Boom!* Just like that. No warning; all I know about this attack is what Dot told me. Of course, these attacks were fits and should have been my biggest if not last warning of what He'd done to me, what He'd made me. Yes, I was a serious alcoholic and if I didn't do something, didn't fight back, I would be a dead alcoholic. Well if you're going to fight back, going to take on the Devil, then what better place to start than the hospital? There even He has no power – well, no physical power, but He still has His mental power.

I was in hospital for two days where I was given vitamin tablets and tablets to lessen the effect of Him being exorcised from my body. Surely now that He had been exorcised from my body and that everybody close to me now knew what I was, I'd be able to lead a normal life and join up with

Him occasionally, like my friends and family did? But like I said, He'd been exorcised from my body but not my brain; up there He'd still be gnawing away at me (still does sometimes) but that didn't matter because I'd been in hospital and been given a clean bill of health, so as far as I was concerned; as long as I saw Him in moderation, I'd be fine. Huh! Moderation! What's that for an alcoholic? Just because I'd spent two days in hospital I thought I was fine, cured. What a load of crap. You're never cured until you die, or almost die. Even with my experience, which I'll talk about later, I still hear His calls for me, except that now they're not so loud.

# CHAPTER
## Seven

WELL, I DID pretty well. I'd resisted His orders for a few months. I was still seeing Him but it was controlled and always out in the open with my mates, never in the seedy, sneaky, secretive way I'd done before. I had appointments at the hospital for an EEG and a cat scan, just to make sure I didn't suffer from epilepsy. The EEG was all clear and so the day of the cat scan I nipped into the pub for a quick pint and bought a packet of Lockets to cover the smell of alcohol. Well, the cat scan was all clear too and a couple of weeks later, the consultant gave me the all clear on my liver and told me I could come off my tablets. This was all great news, so I decided to go for a couple of pints to celebrate on my own. Well, not strictly on my own, because He was there with me. Yep, He'd invited Himself along (cheek).

Now, this going to the pub with just Him started getting more and more frequent, but I saw nothing bad in that. I had Him under control now, I was in charge. What? What the hell was I talking about? *In charge of Satan?* Excuse me, but I don't think so! Well now He'd see another naive sucker and lure him in. Once again, I certainly wasn't the first, and I'm damn sure I won't be the last.

Now He had to go back to work on me, except this time it wouldn't be so hard for Him because I was under the illusion that I was in control now (what a joke) because I'd been given a clean bill of health from the hospital. So now began His second and easier attempt to captivate me.

I say it was easier for the pure fact of my naivety. Yep, I was under the illusion that what happened had happened; He didn't really mean me any harm. Why would He? We were friends – and I thought bloody good friends. Trouble is, He is nobody's friend, He just uses you for His own entertainment and when He's bored, well, it's you who is discarded.

When you're an alcoholic, you're secretive; but no matter how sneaky you are something will happen to you to let out your secret. With me it was the fits, it wasn't just the fact that the doctors knew by their tests, but it was the fact that my mates got me some clothes from my cupboard in my bedroom, and to their shock it wasn't just a jumper or pair of trousers they were pulling out. Oh no! It was empty 3-litre bottles of cider I had stashed away out of anybody's view that had come to my bedroom. So that's how I got rumbled. I was found out because He'd put me somewhere that I couldn't protect Him. So now all my mates knew. Mates! Ha! That's a laugh. Three of them were housemates who just breezed through life and were probably more concerned that they might be losing a drinking partner than trying to help or find out more about my problem. These three – Craig, Darren and Richard – are total wankers, and if one of them was to die tomorrow, my reaction would be one of, 'So?' You see, these three had to be ordered up the hospital to visit me by the best friend I've ever had (except my wife) Derek Groombridge. Dez is the sort of bloke who isn't afraid to ask questions or to give his opinion, but even after one very serious chat with Dez about Him, I still knew deep down I wanted Him back in my life. Even as me and Dez were talking, He'd be going, 'Yeah, yeah, just agree with him and then we'll go about our little way.' You see, He wanted no intruders in our relationship, so that's how it was to be. If anyone talked or discussed my drinking, He'd make me make out that I was more or less teetotal. You see, now I was starting to buy the 3-litre bottles of cider again; yep, same routine of hiding them and so on, and so on, so when I'd go out of a night, I'd only visibly drink about two pints so my mates (who cared) thought I was doing really well. I was never asked if I was drinking secretly again. Probably because they thought that not even I'd be that stupid again. Mind you, if I had been asked, I'd have said, 'No.'

Why start buying the 3-litre bottles of cider again? you might ask. Simple! You see, you'd pay about £2.80 for the 3-litre bottle, while a pint was around £2.20. Now, if I was going to get to my desired destination on pints alone, I'd have to spend about £15 (way over the top), whilst with the cider, I'd be spending under £3 for what would be the equivalent of three to four pints in alcoholic strength. That was the reason for the cider. I'd be saving about £12, look like my drinking was under control and still be at that desired destination.

Yet again there was a change of job for me. I became a postman. I had the interview a few days after the fits and could hardly speak properly because I had bitten my tongue while fitting (very common). I told the interviewers that I had fallen down a couple of stairs and bitten my tongue, to which they were very sympathetic. This interview was done solely on my own; He was banned from this one. I thought to myself that if I could get this job, I could banish Him from my working life, because as a postie, you're more or less your own boss. I thought that as you're on your own for a large part of the day, I wouldn't need His assistance to help me over any hurdles – that's if I got the job of course. I didn't think I would get the job because of how I was at the interview; with my tongue bitten I was talking like a right mong (now my nickname from my wife) but to my joy, about a week later I got the good news. I had got the job and all this was done without Him. Was this now the breakthrough I needed to escape Him? I mean, I had a non-pressurised job, which had an early start. Surely with the early start I wouldn't be able to slip Him down my throat like I had been? There was one major problem with the early start though; it meant an early finish, which meant there was plenty of time for boredom to sink in, which it did. I would be on my own for about five hours till my mates finished work. Well, there I was, a sitting target for Him. I wasn't exactly sitting; I was more like shouting, 'Come on, you bastard, join me!' He did, so I dwindled away those hours with Him by my side.

But even when my mates had got home from work, I didn't ditch Him and go onto the softer drinks, oh no! I carried on seeing Him, but once again in the privacy of my own room. It's strange, though, how He'd make boredom disappear. It was like He'd speed time up. Now, when I'm bored, which is very, very rarely, I get off my ass and find something to do, because as I said to my consultant, 'Boredom is only created by the individual.'

Even though I wasn't drinking before work, I was certainly making up for it after work. Yep, after work the rest of the day was spent with Him. What state my body and mind must have been in at this stage of my life is probably best summed up as: 'He was my body and He was my mind.' It wasn't going to be long before He was going to be needed before I went to work because even though ten times out of ten I'd still be under His influence from the previous day, it would only be a few hours before He'd leave me and I'd be stranded with those feelings of anxiety like I had before the fits. Now I certainly didn't want to fit at work, so I asked Him to join me before I went to work. He obliged. So once again, we were reunited before I went to work. I'd speed round my round so that I could hook up again with Him quicker.

So there it was; day in, day out we were inseparable. Living where I was at the time, I didn't have to be ultra careful or sneaky as I'd be first one home and He'd be hidden up in my room long before anyone else was back from work. This was also the same in my next dwelling (my bedsit), but in my next home I had to be extra careful and sneaky, and there was just one time that I wasn't, and got caught out.

But I still never admitted anything. I was living with a girl who obviously knew nothing about me two-timing her with my best friend until I mistakenly left my waterproof coat unguarded for no more than two hours. Of course, He was occupying the pockets of the coat; she picked it up for some reason and was suspicious of the weight of it. Being a woman, she investigated and of course found Him nestling there safely in my pockets. What a mistake to make. I had realised earlier that I'd left Him there, unguarded, so I had plenty of time to think up a reason as to why there were cans of cider in my postal waterproof. When I got back home and was confronted with what she had found, I never admitted I was an alcoholic (yet again) but merely said there was a group of us who after work, rather than going to the pub, would go to Elizabeth Gardens to down a few cans as it was cheaper. Did she believe me? Didn't know, didn't really care, just as long as she was off my case. It wasn't a long relationship, and when we split up (on very bad terms) she swore to me that she'd be phoning the sorting office to tell them about my little secret. I didn't plead with her not to – God no! That would be showing my guilt. Instead I just said, 'Do whatever you want,' thinking she wouldn't, but you got it. She did! I was lucky though, because it wasn't management who told me about the accusations being thrown around, but a very good friend who I'd previously told what a psycho this girl was. In turn, he had told the managers this, so nothing more was heard of this true allegation.

So there we had it. One stupid mistake could have cost me my job if I were to be found guilty. As it was, this wouldn't have mattered anyway, because due to Him I was throwing more and more sickies. Yep, I had become the world's worse migraine sufferer. A condition I knew quite a lot about as I'd gone out with a sufferer previously. His domination over me was now total and despite a written warning, a verbal warning (which He handled superbly for me) there was no way that my most precious secret was coming out of the bag. So there we had it; my secret or my job. Well, there was only going to be one winner, wasn't there? And despite handing two weeks' notice in, I was, unsurprisingly, sacked after a week's notice had been served. Bit of a shame really, because I was looking forward to the last week's walk to work with Him, a walk in which I thought we'd have no chance of being spotted getting up to our hanky panky but I was. I couldn't believe that when I'd come out of hospital after my stroke, I'd been seen drinking my cans of cider at 5 a.m. in this deserted park. I thought apart from my home, this was a dead cert of a place never to be seen. It didn't matter, because nothing came of it; but it just goes to show that nowhere is safe when you're being devious.

So, once again I was jobless with money running out fast – and I mean fast. My brain's hunger for Him had reached immeasurable levels and I couldn't keep up. I didn't know where I was. The only thing I knew was that wherever I was, I was alone because with the money running out, I had the panic-stricken feeling that He'd be running out on me. So it was decided I'd have to do something I hadn't done, or even thought you could do. My housemate suggested I go to my bank and ask for an overdraft. He said to me that, as I'd been a loyal customer, it would be no problem getting one and how right he was. Of course, I didn't tell him the money was for my way-out-of-control addiction, but that it was for my deposit and first month's rent on my new bedsit. Yeah, after years of moving from Laverstock to Rectory Road, to Bishopdown, to Clifton Row, to Wilton Road, to Pennyfarthing Street, to Harnham, to Dorchester, back to Laverstock, to Bemerton Heath, to Clifton Road, to Elm

Grove Road and finally back to Bemerton Heath, I was in bedsit city again.

Anyway, I got an overdraft of £500. I thought, *Cool! £500. Didn't lift a finger, now I can catch up with Him again and not worry to much about money.* How wrong could I be? You see, the amount of time I was spending with Him, £500 wasn't going to last long, and it wasn't too long before I was back in the bank asking to increase my overdraft. Once again, I managed to get more money without lifting a finger. Although this time it was only £200 and with the warning that this would be my last, and indeed it was. Even though I did try again, I was blankly refused. So there I was, down to my last £50 or so with a friend who had to be fed and clothed. The only money coming in was my paltry Dole money, which was a pathetic amount to keep my friend happy. I knew the overdraft had to be paid back, and I needed to get a job, but these were minor problems in my mind. My main priority was getting money to keep Him happy and keep Him accustomed to the lifestyle He was used to with me. I mean, I didn't want Him to run off with anyone else, did I?

Then a mate, who I'd told about my cash flow problem, suggested I go for a crisis loan. I thought, *Why not?* I mean, I had no chance with the bank. Well, I went to the social office, filled out the crisis loan forms, waited in there for about three hours and received a giro for thirty-odd quid. I thought, *Thirty-odd quid? That's a bit pathetic, but beggars can't be choosers.* Maybe if I'd gone in there with a four-pack of extra strong cider and a dog, I would have got more, if you know what I mean.

Well, this wasn't to be my last visit to social for a crisis loan, God no! There were another three visits, with the amount going down and down. Even social gave up on me and refused me on my fourth visit. Shit! Now what was I to do? I had debt coming out of my ears, but that wasn't my main problem. Nah, fuck the debt; I had to keep my friendship going, and believe me, for a few weeks it was a struggle, but I managed out of my Dole money. No more than £5 was spent on proper food. Nah, you see, he was my food now. I'd think of ways to get a substantial amount of money to keep us happy. Of course, the simplest was to get a job. *Yeah*, I thought, *maybe*. But because I'd been given these handouts from the bank and social, working for money didn't really appeal to me. So I was to do something I certainly never, ever dreamt I would do in my lifetime; I was to ask my brother if I could borrow some much needed cash.

Asking my brother if I could borrow some money off him was one of the lowest and most embarrassing moments of my life. You see, I had always had money, be it by a wage, the bank or social, but now I was really desperate. I knew that if I didn't get any money, He would reap a terrible revenge on me, a revenge much worse than the fits. You see, as silly as it sounds, even I knew I was drinking myself to death, but just couldn't do anything about it. If anything I was speeding up, not slowing down the impending danger to my life. It may sound silly, but I had a certain pride about me that wouldn't cry out for help; rather than ask for help, I'd rather keep quiet and suffer whatever He was to throw at me; if that meant death, then so be it.

Like I said, asking my brother for money was hard but I had to, I had to swallow whatever pride I had, or thought I had. Not being brave enough to ask face to face, I texted my brother with my cash flow problem. I said it was for rent and asked to borrow £200. He texted back saying he'd give me the money when I was up Dot's next. Needless to say, I was up Dot's the next day. I gratefully took the £200 from my brother, and promised he'd get it back when I started to work. Hmm! Work! Yeah, that was something I still wasn't really thinking about, but now I had borrowed money off my brother, I knew I'd start looking. I had to get a job now. You see, he's my big brother, he'd helped me out and I was certainly not going to let him down. Only problem was though, it was one thing looking for a job, and another thing getting one so from the time I got the first loan from my brother, to the first time I got a wage in my new job, I had asked my brother for another two loans. In all, it totalled up to £400 that I owed him (of which I still owe £50, and he'll get).

Out of all the debt I was in, my brother's was the most important for me to pay off. The bank and social – ha! Stuff them; they can wait till I'm ready, not them. My brother is my family and much more important than a building. Well anyway, I did get a job, a job back in the catering trade and believe me it didn't feel half good getting my first wage and paying my brother back some of his money, and of course having money coming in weekly to keep the ongoing friendship with Him.

Of course, with weekly pay, you don't have worries about how you're going to keep up your very private life. My wage was mine, and now nobody had to be asked if they could lend me some money. It was going to be Him and me for ever. With a new job, was I going to sort myself out? Try and wrestle myself away from His grasp? Poo! Was I hell! I had a wage coming in now; I didn't have to limit myself so much. All I had to do was work out my drinking strategy on the way to work.

Well, my strategy was pretty simple. I'd wake up, He'd be down by my side, and I'd drink at least a litre of His blood or another way of putting it, my wake-up juice. I'd leave for work looking well up for the day ahead and before getting to work I'd gulp down another can under the subway, and a final can in a secluded car park near to my workplace. In my jacket were two cans of Frosty Jack's for when I got out of work, as I'd need a hit of His power, because His earlier magic would be starting to fade away. These two cans were quickly downed in the bus station toilets; might not have been the most glamorous setting for our date, but me and Him didn't mind because we were behind a locked door, very private. Just deviating a little. The cans in the pocket and taken to work was a very risky move, as I found out in hospital when a workmate said to me that the boss wanted to see me to ask if I'd been drinking at work. The kitchen porter had found my two little demons in my coat pocket. What the kitchen porter was doing in my coat pocket, I will never know, but the cans were most definitely for after work. After the amount I'd drunk before going to work, there was no way that I was going to drink any more at work. Jesus, no! A kitchen is a dangerous place to work at the best of times, but totally out of your head would be suicide; not just for me, but also for my workmates. As it was, my job was ended there because of the stroke.

Anyway, back to more important things. Just before getting this new job, I was still going out on the town, despite the fact I was limited to a very tight budget. You see, the money I had borrowed from the bank, social, my brother was mainly for my bottles and cans, but I'd still go out. I just wouldn't drink as much in a pub, firstly, because it would've been too expensive, and secondly, I was pretty well tanked up from the bottles and cans I'd drunk before going out.

Well, it was on one of these nights out that I met a girl who I was going to cause a lot of heartache for. On this night, I met a girl called Debby Freeman. Deb's really good looking, and naturally that's the first thing that attracted me to her. I can't understand when you ask somebody, 'What's the first thing you look for in a woman?' and they say, 'First thing I look for is a good personality.' Rubbish! You see, the first thing you look for in a woman when you're in a pub or club is how attractive she is. Looks first, personality second, that's my opinion. If you get a combination of both, as I have with Debby, then you're a very lucky bloke.

Obviously this was the first time I'd seen Deb, and we'd been eyeing each other up. We were in a group of people we both knew and started chatting. Now this was where I saw the personality side of her coming through. Good looks, good personality, should I go for it? Of course I should. You see, I think we have another sense that kicks in, in a situation like this, telling us, 'Go on then, what you waiting for? You're attracted to her, she's attracted to you, what you waiting for?' Well, I was eighty-five per cent sure that

Deb was attracted to me in the same way that I was to her, so in a brave move I said to her, 'You've got nice looking lips, do you mind if I kiss them?' What was coming next was either going to be a slap or, well I don't know what. As it was, Deb replied with, 'I've forgotten how to,' to which I replied, 'Let me remind you,' and *boom!* That was it, except there was a small problem of me seeing another girl. Well, I say seeing; it was never and was never going to be anything serious. Even though Deb and me had shared that first kiss, it was still going to be another month before we became boyfriend and girlfriend. Why? Probably because I still had Him, who at this stage of my life was the most important thing and, of course, the little matter of ditching this other girl I was sort of seeing. Well, the ditching of her wasn't too hard as she had me arrested for sending threatening text messages, all caused because the stupid cow had dumped all my clothes outside my best mate's house because of some tiff, and do you know what night I got arrested? The night I got arrested was the first night I was going to go up to Debby's house!

# CHAPTER
## Eight

I WAS KEPT IN the police station for about four hours. Now that was bloody hard, I was on my own; He was back at the bedsit waiting for me. I had all the routine stuff done at the station. You know, questions, photos taken, fingerprints and so on, and was let off with a caution, thank God! Good job as well, because I would have dreaded to see the state I would have been in if I had to spend a whole night away from Him.

Well, when I did get out, I must have done the quickest half-mile in history to get back to my place from the police station. I phoned Debby up to explain what had happened, which she was cool about, and proceeded to unscrew His head and gulp down from His perfect body (full bottle) and I promised to Him and myself that apart from sleeping, I'd never be away from Him for so long.

As time went on, Deb and me got more and more serious and we decided I would move in with her. Yeah, definitely a good idea. Move in with my girlfriend, get to know each other better and be like a family. Me, Deb, David and Ben (Deb's two sons). Of course, moving from the bedsit where there was no chance of anybody interrupting me and Him, to a maisonette where there was a family living meant there had to be radical changes in my planning of meeting up with Him. I mean, it was never an issue now of new girlfriend, new place

*Return Ticket Please*

to live, how about ditching a friend? No chance! We'd just have to be ultra careful from now on.

A lot of you might say, 'Well, with all the drinking you were doing, how come Deb never smelt it on you?' Well the only answer I can give to that is Lockets. Yep, Lockets. You see, to conceal my obvious alcohol breath, I'd suck on Lockets. Yep and not just one, God no! I was going through about two packets a day. I had either the original ones or the blackcurrant ones. The blackcurrant ones were better tasting, but the originals seemed to mask my breath better, so with the blackcurrant ones I'd double up with some chewing gum. My God, since my stroke, I haven't even looked at a Locket, let alone sucked one. Tell you what; their shares must have gone down. I'll always remember my best mate, Des, saying to me after my stroke, that it was a bit obvious about my drinking; I mean, who has a cold the whole summer? Anyway, that's why Deb never knew, so now that my breath wasn't a problem, I had to devise a plan to get Him, hide Him and meet Him. The plan was going to involve a certain amount of risk taking, as does every secretive plan. So to keep up my addiction after I bought my stash, I'd stuff it in a bush outside the block of flats where we lived. The items contained in my bag of goodies would be the 3-litre bottle of cider and three cans of cider. It was like Santa's Christmas sack, but this one certainly wasn't for kids. Sometimes there would be more but never less.

Now He had His hiding place, which in itself was a risk; not so much because Deb might find it, but because of the area we lived in. You see, it was one of them areas that if somebody knew there was a free bit of alcohol hanging about, they'd take it. This actually did happen once, which infuriated me so I decided to throw another sickie. Yeah, I was at the stage that there was no way I was going to work without His blood running through my veins.

Now that I had His hiding place sorted, I had to think of the next stage of my operation, which was to see Him before I even got on the bus for work. Now this was a little bit trickier as Deb started work at more or less the same time as me, so naturally you'd think we would get the same bus. But no, I would insist that Deb get the earlier bus so that I could have a little bit of time to myself. Of course, my little bit of time to myself was spent with another. Not another woman, as I later found out was what Deb thought, but my master. So this would be the final part of my operation. God, most of my adult life it seems I've been planning, scheming, ducking and diving and all for Him. Well, I'd see Deb off to work on her bus, and then run down to the bush to release Him of His imprisonment.

Once He was released, I was relieved of my overwhelming need for Him. God knows how much of His blood I would drink before the bus came round, but however much was left, I'd hide back in the bush ready for me to guzzle down after work. Now this was the first part of my 'drinkathon' before work. The second part was gulping down another two of His little counterparts that I had with me. They'd be consumed in my workplace car park in a very secretive corner. That was it, I was done, and I was alive, awake and ready for anything, another day and anything that work could throw at me (c'mon!). I'd breeze into work, mind and body where it wanted to be, breath freshened with my lockets and coat pockets filled with a couple of my little demons for straight after work. This was every working day. It was perfect, it was strategic, and it was bulletproof. Firstly, because no little detail was ignored, and secondly if you think about it, how many people are really going to ask if you've been drinking before work? I mean, these people are your workmates, things like a colleague being an alcoholic and drinking before work doesn't happen where you work, it happens in other workplaces; be careful it could be happening right on your doorstep. I, myself, couldn't even say one hundred per cent if somebody was an alcoholic, solely because of how conniving I was (course, I could tell a street wino) and anyway, if somebody is brave enough to ask if you've been drinking before work, you just fall back on the old 'course not but I had a hell of a session last night' excuse.

Well, my drinking was not out of control; my drinking was my life, apart from some other bits thrown in. There were now times that I'd always have a can in my pocket, whether it be at home, in town, round my mates', cinema, restaurant, even in a pub. I mean, for God sake! In a pub? They sell the bloody stuff. But yeah, I'd nip into the toilet as soon as getting to the pub, get Him out of my trouser pocket, gulp Him down, crush Him and stuff Him behind the cistern before going onto the much weaker garbage served in the pub. Whilst Him and me were having so much fun, everyone else took a back seat, I guess; parents, brother, friends and, of course Deb. I mean, I'd never, ever have said I'd lied to Deb about all this, but deceive her; yes, definitely. For example, there was a time I'd come out of the off-license and saw her walking my way, so in a controlled state of panic, I quickly turned round and walked the other way, pretending not to see her. I mean, if I'd stopped to talk, it would have been just me she was seeing, not me and Him. Of course, with this suspicious bit of behaviour, it reinforced in her head that I must be seeing someone else. Understandable, but no way, babe.

Anyway, me and Deb were getting more and more serious. Only problem was, though, how serious can or do you get when you've got Him as your best friend? Well anyway, in my state of mind, I thought it was serious. But was it serious enough to tell Deb about my dark secret? Simple answer to that is no, but you must believe me when I say I came to within a millimetre of telling her on several occasions. You have to understand the decision to tell her wasn't in my hands, it was all in His. So every time I thought I'd plucked up the courage to tell her, He'd be gnawing away in my head with the simple question of, 'Why?'

'Why? I'm in love with the girl, she has the right to know about this.'

He'd come back with, 'Would she be able to handle it? And whether she could or couldn't, would she stand by you?' I don't know.

Well, whatever reasons I'd come up with for why Deb had to know, He'd counteract them with a much better reason for not telling her. I was lost and would think about how I could tell Deb in a way, but not tell her, if you know what I mean. You know, in a riddle sort of way, or, in other words, the bottler's way. So I decided (don't know when this wasn't planned) that I'd tell Deb that I knew I'd be dead by the time I was thirty-five (close). You know, in a jokey but very serious manner.

Well, of course, Deb took it with a pinch of salt at first, but I think the more and more I dropped it into conversation, she got upset so I thought to myself I had better stop saying it. Anyway, as far as He was concerned, I'd already said too much but He let me off because in all reality, how was Deb going to work out that what I was saying was remotely connected to alcohol? Of course she'd ask what the hell I meant about it, but I'd just say, 'Oh it's like a sixth sense, I just get this strong feeling that's going to happen.' So in a way, even though I knew I was out of control, I wasn't getting better, but worse and I wasn't trying or even interested in doing anything about it, so in a peculiar sort of way, I was committing a suicide bid; all be it a long-term bid, a bid it is. I mean, of course it's suicidal. Alcohol is OK in moderation, but in vast amounts you're trying to kill yourself. Once again, you are doing it slowly and probably enjoying it seventy-five per cent of the time, but do you really know what's happening inside your body? Of course not, even if you get the warning signs as I did (fits), you, as I did, will probably go back to the old sauce. Not everybody, of course; only the weak-willed like myself.

So now my suicide mission was well underway. I was pissed, but not pissed every day of the week, if you know what I mean. I was happy and not hurting anybody apart from myself; I wasn't lying to anybody apart from, once again, myself.

I was occasionally letting other people take the blame for my drinking, as was one such case when Deb had a bottle of

Cinzano and had left it downstairs. There was probably about three-quarters of the bottle left when I'd nip downstairs and start taking large gulps out of it, thus leaving about a quarter of a bottle left. Deb's assumption was that her son David must have been swigging out of it. He pleaded his innocence, but Deb wasn't having it. She told me, and I tried to help him as best I could, by saying that I didn't think he had, I mean you were knocking it back pretty hard last night. Whether she believed David's cry of innocence back then or not she certainly does now. Anyway, it was too late for me to try and get help now. For one I was too stubborn, and secondly I was too scared. So something had to happen, something bad, something so bad it'd either kill me or turn my life upside down. It would have to be something out of this world to banish the demon who had controlled my life for all those years. Well, believe me, when it came I think some days dying would have been the easier option!

So what was it? What was going to rid me of the Devil? Well, as I said earlier, I had a brain haemorrhage (stroke). It's funny. Once again, you'd think, 'Blimey, a stroke, he'll never remember anything about that,' but I do, believe me I do. It happened on 2 March 2003, almost a year to the day as I write this extract. Anyway, Deb and me had gone to bed, obviously there were three of us in bed. Deb, me and, of course, Him. Just a quick deviation: my best mate Des said to sell a book you need sex, plenty of sex in it. Well, I'm afraid to say the only sex you're getting in this book, is that me and Deb were in bed that fateful night and getting fruity when all of a sudden it happened!

I was sat on the bed, ready for you know what, when all

of a sudden, *Kaboom!* there was a massive explosion in my head. I can tell you it was the worst pain I've ever felt in my life. Well, I wasn't panicky at all; I just went to stand up when 'flop', I fell off the bed. I tried to get back up but for some reason I couldn't; my legs and arms just weren't doing anything, and although this was happening, still there was no panic. I just said to Deb, 'I've got a migraine, get me some Anadin,' although you know what my brain was saying: 'It's Him you need, not Anadin.' Well whether it was Him I needed or not, He wasn't going to be my rescuer, oh no! On this occasion He was the villain.

Well, what happened next is what I've been told by Deb because the next time I woke up I was in hospital. The Anadin did their job, I s'pose, 'cause mixed with the alcohol in my body, I must have fallen asleep and the next time I could remember anything I didn't have a headache. So after these strange happenings, you'd think He'd done enough damage to me, but no; He wanted to inflict more punishment on me. Once again, this next part is as told by Deb, as is much of this passage.

When Deb woke up, I was sweating and breathing weirdly and then out of nowhere, with no warning, I fitted. Well, this caused obvious panic and confusion in Deb because to see someone fit is not a pretty sight, especially if you've never witnessed one before and especially if it's a loved one. Well, Deb rang for an ambulance and Tina, a friend of ours who is a nurse and who lived close to us. Tina obviously got there before the ambulance, and I was still fitting, but had calmed down a bit, so Tina put me in the recovery position. I remember Deb saying that she didn't even know to do that. Well, let me ask this, how many people who read this would? Just imagine your boyfriend is fitting, you don't know why, you're panicking, your mind's a mess, would anybody who is not qualified in medicine think, *Right, recovery position!* I think not, or even if they did, would they know how to get the patient into the position? I tell you something, I might think it but I wouldn't have a clue how to get them into the recovery position!

Anyway, the ambulance got there and I started fitting again, quite badly. They sedated me and rushed me to Salisbury District Hospital. It was here that they did tests and told Deb, Dot, Frank and my brother that I had to be rushed to Southampton General Hospital for an emergency brain operation and that I could die. Well, I was in the theatre for about four and a half hours and, as Deb put it, they were the longest in her life. Well, you'd think with all the shenanigans of the night before, I'd be in a pretty shit state; well I can't really remember much of the next few weeks. Once again, this is all from Deb, but even though I can't remember anything, Deb has told me that when she came the day after, I muttered the words 'I love you,' even though I couldn't remember who she was!

Well, that is just one of the things Deb has told me that happened in those days at Southampton where my mind was just a blank. I've said to Deb on several occasions that I would have loved to have videoed the goings on at Southampton where it seems I got up to some pretty peculiar things. Nothing seemed to be functioning in my brain, and when the doctors asked me what year it was, for some reason my answer would be 1997! As Deb has said to me, the person she was visiting in hospital wasn't me. I mean, I didn't even know her. I seemed to know everyone else just not my girlfriend. I couldn't begin to imagine how much that hurt, but why? Why was it Deb I didn't recognise? In a weird, haunting sort of way, was this His way of telling me that Deb was the one for me? You know, was He telling me, 'I've done my damage to you and you've survived. Now it's someone else's turn to take you on.' Well if it was, He shouldn't have bothered to damage me, because I already knew that Deb was going to be very special.

Anyway, if it wasn't enough for Deb that I didn't know her, the next thing she was going to find out was going to be quite a shock. You see, the next thing she was to find out was about Him and me; yeah, Deb was to find out the basics of me being an alcoholic. Just the basics – more was to come out later from me. I don't know how the doctors could tell I was an alcoholic, but they did. Although when I was moved to Salisbury Hospital, they were under the assumption that the stroke was caused by binge drinking. More like 24/7 drinking.

Well, back to Deb finding out about Him and me. Obviously, having had the surgery, I was receiving drugs for my recovery. It was these drugs that Deb assumed were making me behave weirdly. Well it wasn't the drugs; it was, of course, the DTs. According to Deb, my weird behaviour included doing my job, yeah in my confused, out of this world mode, I was chopping up carrots, putting them into a saucepan and mumbling under my breath that I had to go quicker or I'd get into trouble. I mean, what the fuck is that all about? I'll tell you what its all about, it's about Him being exorcised from me. It was during these times of the DTs that Deb was asked by the doctor if she knew what she was letting herself in for. Well yeah, I think she did, and as far as Deb was concerned, it was a case of getting my head sorted out then the booze, 'cause let's face it, I wasn't even going to think about drink for a while, if at all. Well, in Southampton, I was quite amazing! I mean, I'd fallen out of bed and it had taken six big blokes to pick me up. I told Des that I'd been to get some cranberry sauce; I even thought Des and Deb were going out with each other as I told them what a lovely couple they made. I was in a totally different world, my world.

I spent three weeks in Southampton and I can't remember a single thing. I can't remember a visitor, a doctor, a nurse, eating a meal or another patient. Basically, three weeks of my life has been erased from my memory! I can't even remember being transported back to Salisbury Hospital, which was to become my home for the next eight weeks and out of those eight weeks, the first couple are also a blur as I was still in my own little world and still in 1997. So again, the next few bits of the book are from what Deb has told me.

Well, the first ward I was put on in Salisbury was Woodford Ward and is a mixed ward. I wouldn't have thought so when Deb told me what I was doing one day. Yeah, there I was one day in Woodford, laid in my bed quite happily just flashing all my privates to all. Of course I didn't know I was doing this, but still it must have been a shock to the other patients, most of whom were on the older side. In Woodford, it just wasn't me. I was pulling the tubes out of my head, telling the doctors that they weren't shoving a suppository up my arse, 'cause I ain't no chutney ferret chaser. I even told Deb one time that she had to leave because my girlfriend was coming, thinking I was going out with one of the nurses.

# CHAPTER
# Nine

LOOKING BACK, this all seems very funny, and it is, but there was a lot of hard work ahead, and I mean hard work, because having a stroke means your brain has been damaged or killed off on one side. So this means you have to learn how to walk, how to get your arm back into action, and also how to do the simplest of tasks again. I'll tell you what, it's not all plain sailing. Some people might think you've got a cushy life because you ain't in the routine of the real world. I ask those people to think again. Which would you prefer, your safe daily routine or starting a journey to get you back into the real world?

Anyway, this hard work was to come, and if they were telling me on Woodford Ward what was lying ahead of me, it certainly wasn't registering in my brain at first, but slowly and surely it was, as were other things. One day I got the year right and, as Deb put it, that was the breakthrough point. I remembered the year, where I was and, most importantly, I remembered Deb. All was explained about what had happened to me and I took that very calmly, having the attitude of 'what's happened has happened, things can only get better'. I do remember saying to Deb though, that I'd be back to work in a week so; even though I'd been told what had happened, I don't think it had really sunk in, but when it finally did sink in, I was still very calm.

Only on one occasion do I remember it getting me down as one day I said to Deb that I'd never get out of hospital. She assured me that I would, so that was good enough for me. On Woodford Ward, as things were getting clearer in my head, so was what He had done to me and also the fact that now this had happened everybody around me who I knew now knew about my secret affair with Him. But more importantly, the most important person in my life (Deb) now knew. How would she react? (More later.) People knew it was, and was going to be, a hard time for me, but it was also going to be a hard time for Deb, probably worse. For a start, Deb was getting a lot of grief off Dot, and the only reason I can think of for that is that, of course, Dot was hurting and worried, and couldn't take it out on Frank or my brother, so Deb was an easy target. Well, for whatever reason, she was being how she was, it was wrong. It was doing nobody any good and was certainly not aiding my rehabilitation. In fact, her behaviour resulted in me having a go at her for being rude to Deb. This resulted in her refusing to come up and see me until I apologised (excuse me?). Well, I never did, out of sheer stubbornness. (She came up again.)

Well, I've said that things were getting clearer in my head, which they were, but occasionally I was still in my own little world. Like, for example, the day I told Frank and Deb that I'd been outside and had a couple of fags and that I'd also had my wallet stolen! Oh yeah, and let's not forget the day that I told Deb I was coming home tomorrow! (I wished.) Then there was a time when I just shot up in the bed and shouted out, 'God! This stroke thing does nothing for your sex drive!' Sex! Well, it was obviously nothing I was really thinking of at this time, well not in my real mind, but it seems it was on my subconscious mind. The subject of sex became more prominent as I got better and better, and let me tell you, there were a couple of worrying moments as I wasn't feeling a twinge down in the 'old boy' for a couple of weeks. But as time wore on, the old chap became aware of his existence and soon perked up to his full magnificence! Quite funny about sex and a stroke, because nine times out of ten, one of the first questions asked by people after they've gone through the pleasantries of, 'How are you?' is, 'Can you still have sex?' Well, I'm not a prude and I can one hundred per cent tell you that, 'Yes, you can.'

My time on Woodford Ward was drawing to an end after a couple of weeks. Yep, it had been two weeks of lying in bed, muttering utter garbage to my visitors and generally not remembering much; sounds like a Sunday morning after being out on the piss the night before. Well, what I can remember of being on Woodford? Not much. I can say I enjoyed, but now it was over it was on to the next part of my rehabilitation, and this meant being moved to Farley Ward and this is where the hard work was to begin. Farley Ward meant physio and occupational therapy!

I didn't really know what I was in for with this physio and occupational therapy. Yeah, I knew that it was to get me learning how to walk, use my left arm and basically make my brain aware that I do have a left side, but how, how were the physios and OTs going to make somebody who had to be lifted to a wheelchair to go to the toilet, have his arse wiped, be shaved, have his food cut up, regain awareness of his left-hand side? Hard work, and a bloody lot of it. But in the end it all came down to me; yeah, me the individual. If the individual isn't in the right frame of mind and is feeling sorry for themselves, then forget it. Mind you, you could probably see how someone might get like that when moving to Farley Ward. I was obviously nervous, as was Deb, and my nerves were understandable as my first experience was a man called Brian, just sitting on his bed, staring aimlessly into space with dribble running down his chin. God! Even though Deb was there, I knew she wouldn't be all the time, and God did I feel lonely. Even though I felt like that on the inside, on the outside I would still have a joke and laugh. You have to, otherwise that feeling sorry for yourself crap comes in and like I said, if that happens, forget it.

So to my rehab! It would be impossible to go through every part of my rehab, but there is one thing I learned pretty quickly and that was to achieve anything, I had to visualise it in my brain. If it were visualised, it would make the task easier. You see, this visualisation was the undamaged part of my brain taking over the duties of my damaged part.

Anyway, on Farley I had, of course, highs and lows (mainly highs) and it may be boring to read, but I'll share them with you anyway.

My first aim in Farley was the walking side of my rehab. The physios and OTs were obviously keen to bring the walking and arm side of it along together, but I must admit, I was more concerned about my walking and somewhat neglected my arm. The first thing I had to get into my brain was to have the confidence in myself and my left leg, that it was there and did have a purpose. Now this was going to be bloody hard. I mean, the poor thing hadn't moved in about a month, and with the added problem of my brain not even knowing it was there, it may seem like a lost cause. But no! With skilled physios, who were absolutely brilliant, I began a programmed, detailed course of exercise. Not too much, as I got tired very quickly and my concentration span at that time was, at most, half an hour, and not too little as we wanted to make progress. I would start my physio by being helped into my wheelchair and transported to the gym. Even this little task of being helped into the wheelchair was helping me, because it was making the brain aware of my leg so we were getting results already. So now that my leg is realising it was there, we had to press on so now the physics wanted me to sit on the bed and stand up with them – of course, with one on each side of me. Now, this was a very nerve-racking experience, because straight away the brain was thinking, *Shit we're going to fall*. So immediately, without me realising, all my weight was going through my right hand side. Of course this was going to happen. The right was unaffected and my brain was going to stand me up in the safest way possible. This, to me, was a minor problem, and anyway I was standing. I was proud of myself! Too bloody right I was! Yeah, it was an aided, very unsteady stand, but a stand it was. I couldn't wait to tell Deb what I had achieved in physio. She was proud of me, and even though I had immense determination to crack this walking lark, knowing that Deb was proud of me and one hundred per cent behind me, gave me even more determination.

Things were going good and looking up. In fact, things

were going so good, that I'll never forget the day that I opened a Twix bar. Jesus Christ, the excitement in telling Deb was bordering on the verge of orgasmic. With things going so well there was always in the back of my mind that, 'OK, now what's going to go wrong?' Well I'll tell you what was going wrong; Dot, that's what was going wrong. She was still being horrible to Deb, thus causing another falling out with me, thus causing me more stress. Why on earth she was being like this I'll never know. I've asked, but I've never had a proper answer. Instead of being like this she should have been supporting Deb. Even though this was on my mind, I had to block it out because, not trying to sound selfish, ninety-nine per cent of what was happening now was about me.

Well anyway, like I said, physio was going good and I'll come back to physio in a bit because now that I was with it, the subject of Him was looming on the horizon and me and Deb had to talk about it. So soon would be the time for me to confess all my sins to Deb and tell her about my secret affair with my friend from hell...

*CHAPTER*
## Ten

THE DAY HAD come. With the assistance of the nurses I got into the wheelchair and Deb wheeled me out onto the little green. Well, we both knew what we were here for; it was time for me to grass Him up to the woman I loved. Was I nervous? A little bit! But at the end of the day, there were only two possible reactions from Deb; either she would support me and stay by my side and beat Him out of my life, or she would wash her hands of me and get on with her life without the millstone of me around her neck. Thankfully she chose the first. If she had chosen the second, I'm not saying for sure I'd be dead now, but let's just put it this way: He would've won.

Well, how would Deb take hearing from me that what the doctors had said at Southampton was true, that I was an alcoholic? Would she scream, faint, shout? Well, it was none of these. Her reaction was one of total shock, total amazement, amazement that for all this time I had been keeping my addiction hidden from her. Once again that came down to discipline and immaculate planning. Deb said herself that the only clue she'd had that I was an alcoholic was after the stroke and she'd found two cans of cider in my coat pocket, but by then, it was too late; He'd done his damage.

Now that Deb knew I was an alcoholic, I think in a strange way it put her mind at rest because now she could understand some of my secretive and weird behaviour. Now she knew I wasn't seeing another woman all them times I wanted to be on my own, I was seeing Him. Anyway, we talked and, of course, my immediate answer to the question of are you going to stop drinking – well not so much 'are you going to stop' but 'you have to stop' – was, 'Yes I know I do and I will!' This was a very easy thing to say in the safe grounds of the hospital, but what about in the outside world? Well, to that I answer still to this day, 'I ain't going back to Him!' But you never know because the line is so fine. When Deb and me talked I think He did have one more go to try and get back into me. There was a time I said to Deb, 'Leave me, you're better off without me.' Whether I meant this or not is unknown, but my strong belief is that it was one more last-ditch effort from Him to reunite the two of us. Well, whatever I said that for it didn't matter and Deb showed me what true love is by staying. I mean, she never knew what I was when we first met but she did now. Many a woman would have left, and believe me, I know a few weak, pathetic ones who would have, but no! Deb stayed and I love her immensely.

Well, Deb and me knew the alcohol thing was going to be as much if not more of a struggle as my physio, but we knew that we'd get through it if I was honest. I was still working hard at physio, which I'll come back to, but you see I had another problem: smoking.

Yeah, smoking. You see, before the stroke I was a thirty-plus a day smoker, so this was probably another thing that contributed to the stroke. Now in Southampton and Woodford I hadn't even thought about having a ciggie, but on Farley, where my mind was starting to get back on track, I started to get urges for one. I told this to Deb and she had a word with a nurse who gave me some patches. Now I wasn't one hundred per cent for giving up, as you should be when trying to, but I tried the patches and they seemed to be working. The only time I really thought about a ciggie was in the morning and when I went out in the wheelchair with Deb and she sparked up. Other than those two times of the day, I was fine. Then, after about a week into my giving up smoking, I started to get really bad pains in my chest. God, they were so bad I could hardly move. I was put on some antibiotics – yeah, more tablets added to the thirty-one I was taking a day. I was having blood tests three times a day and even a CAT scan, which worried Deb cause she thought there was something wrong in my head again.

Well, after a week of these tests, I was diagnosed as having pneumonia. I couldn't believe it. I mean, you see all this stuff about trying to give up and this happens! Now the problem was known, it was treated accordingly. I had been in hospital for about five weeks at this stage and hadn't had a cigarette, which was the longest ever for me. I said all this time that this was my best chance of giving up, but like I said, my heart wasn't one hundred per cent into it and I knew, as did Deb, that when I got out of hospital, I would start again and I did. I can honestly say I don't want to give up now. I had my best chance in hospital and that's gone now. Anyway, I've had to give Him up and he was a massive part of my life; I need one vice. When I wasn't smoking in hospital, Deb tried to support me and gave up herself for about a day. Well, never mind, at least the thought was there, babe.

As I was more or less bedridden for a week, my physio had been put on hold, but once I was fit again I was ready and eager to give it more than one hundred per cent. Well, I was back to physio and was up for it when another problem was recognised. This problem wouldn't affect my physio but as it turned out it would affect a part of my sight. You see, when the doctors would do their tests of moving their finger from the side of my head and asking me when I could see it, they noticed that I wasn't noticing the finger till it was more or less in front of me. So it turned out I had paralific vision, or rugby ball vision. I was told by a doctor that it was caused by a film of blood over my eye caused by the operation. An optician has since told me that it's happened because the sight part of my brain had been damaged by the stroke. I know this is a minor problem and loads of people have it, but at thirty-two and with good eyesight (or so I thought) it came as a bit of a shock and took a bit of adapting to. I mean, nothing major has been broken in shops but things have been knocked off shelves and more cups have been broken at home. As I said, I thought my eyesight was good, but a visit to the optician showed me that I need glasses, so now I wear them. They don't help my paralific vision but boy, do I need them.

Anyway, these were minor problems, the pneumonia and the vision. I had much bigger problems and obstacles to conquer. I was ready to jump – well, not jump – back into physio – you know what I mean. So in physio it was time to progress on my rehab. I'd stood with assistance, so now it was time to get onto the parallel bars and get my left leg moving. Now, in my week off, I'd actually visualised this in my brain so I had convinced myself that I could do it but there was a problem because visualising it was one thing, but having the courage to do it was another because as my physio put it, 'When you're a child and running around, you don't care if you fall over in front of a crowd of people, it's expected, but when you're an adult it's embarrassing if you fall over.' Well, with this in mind, it was hard to pluck up the courage but I knew I had to. When I did pluck up the courage it was all down to that 'fuck it' moment – you know, that feeling that just hits you in a trying situation. Well, I had reached the 'fuck it' moment and with my physics on either side of me, I gingerly moved up from my wheelchair and with both hands out I speedily grasped hold of the bar (success). Wow, man! Result! But this was only the first part done. Next the physics wanted me to step ahead with my left leg. Of course I was holding on to the bars with all my strength. You see, my brain knew what danger might lie ahead and was making my left arm work without me knowing. (White-knuckle stuff.)

Well, here it was, my first step for about six weeks. Now six weeks may not seem long considering some sports injuries, but this was a brain injury, not a broken leg. There it was, I'd done it! Absolutely amazing. Yeah, all my weight was on my right hand side, but I didn't care about that, because I was getting closer and closer to something that in Southampton they said I'd never do again. Walk! And even more excitement in myself was that as I stepped with my left, I could actually visualise that my right leg was following and I was walking normally (excellent). There was of course the excitement of telling Deb, Dot, dad and brother and any other visitors. I don't know how much this meant to any of them because it was an everyday thing with them, but to me it was bloody marvellous.

I always wished in physio that I could do more and the sessions would last longer, but it just wasn't possible because being a stroke victim I would get tired very easily just by doing my stand-ups and my little bit of walking. As each physio session continued my confidence in my left leg got better so now I was in the bars and taking my hands off – only for a few seconds and not with the physics by my side; the bars were now my insurance against injury. In physio you can't dawdle on things you've done in the past like your standing up and first step so things move on pretty quickly. This is early stage physio; the more intricate physio comes when you've left hospital and are back at home.

So now I was starting to master the very basics of learning how to walk again, my next challenge was looming and this was a challenge that inside myself I was shitting myself about. I don't think anyone realised how much because I never told them, but believe me I was crapping it. The next challenge for me was to start using a walking frame. Yeah, like I said I was crapping it, but my fear wasn't going to overcome my determination. The walking frame fear had to and would be conquered. I'd seen other patients using them and it looked pretty easy, but this wasn't other patients now, it was *me*.

Like I said, physio was moving along quickly now. I think the speed at which the physics were doing my physio programme was down to my age. I mean, at thirty-two you shouldn't be cooped up in hospital after a brain haemorrhage and learning how to walk again and use your left-hand side; no, you should be working and enjoying life. Well, it may seem hard to believe but I *was* enjoying life; I mean, I was achieving more than I ever did or would at work and I was beating more challenges in a day than a lot of people at work would ever in a lifetime.

And as I've said, the next challenge was here; the walking frame. If – no, not if, but *when* – I mastered the walking frame I knew I'd be half way to regaining my independence to walk on my own again (with walking stick). I was wheeled down to the gym to have my first go on the frame. I got up out of my wheelchair and quickly grabbed onto the frame and I'll tell you what, it didn't half feel bloody good; there I was, standing up feeling proud inside myself – yeah, too damn right I was feeling proud. I wasn't looking for a standing ovation or anything like that from the physics because I was giving one to my bloody self inside my head (too right).

Well, I'm standing there what next? Move your leg, Derek, come on now, you can do it, you're safe, your hands are squeezing the frame so hard I'm surprised the bars aren't bending. Here we go then, *Boom!* Left leg's moved, I'm steady, make sure hands are tight on bars now bring right leg along, yes done it, now move frame a little bit and repeat procedure. Excellent, I'm doing it, I'm walking, I'm f***ing walking! Well, I was chuffed to bits and was a little disappointed when my session had come to an end. I didn't voice my disappointment and knew the physics knew I was tired and I knew I was too. And anyway, learning how to walk again had to be done properly and when I was tired or my concentration had gone there was no point in carrying on; as they say, Rome wasn't built in a day, and I knew I'd be back tomorrow.

Well, this was my biggest achievement by far and once again I couldn't wait to tell my nearest and dearest. Once again there were the congratulations and well dones from everybody, which gave me even more determination. It's quite weird with the determination thing, because it didn't seem that I was consciously telling myself to conquer the challenges that were being put in front of me, it just seemed to be happening – well, happening with the walking at least; my left arm was a totally different kettle of fish. I don't know why, but things just didn't seem to be happening with my left arm; I do know why, it was just simply that I didn't seem interested in it. Oh don't get me wrong, it was used as a very last resort; I mean, if I had something to pick up if I could've used my mouth rather than my left arm I would've. Of course the OTs had seen the lack of effort I was putting in to my left arm and would give me a telling off. But you see, apart from my occupational therapy my left arm would more or less be redundant. Even when it came to mealtimes I would order something that I'd be able to eat with my right hand only. You see, the problem was I hadn't visualised me using my left arm yet, so if I haven't done that yet then no amount of prompting or nagging is going to make me use it at every opportunity. The only times I would use it would be in OT when under the scrutiny of the OTs; any other time I would be right-handed, no left hand. I knew in myself that I would visualise it, it was just a case of when.

Well, obviously I *did* visualise it and when this happened I started to use it more, but as I used to say to the OTs, some of the tasks I was asked to do I wouldn't have used my left arm for before the stroke so how was I supposed to do it now? Well, my views were met with a response of, 'Just try it'. Fair enough, I would try it and that trying of things that I wouldn't normally do with my left arm paid off and soon, not straight away, I started becoming more independent with my left arm. For example, I was still being shaved and having my arse wiped, which you don't want for too long, so with the humiliation of that and my visualising of my left arm working, along came my determination. I knew it wouldn't be long before I was shaving myself and doing my own arse wiping. Everything was progressing nicely, I was even visualising in my brain that I was walking without the walking frame. Now that was exciting, but a bit too early to physically achieve it; still, whatever; it was good news.

It must have been around this time that I had my first bath in God knows how long; yet another new experience as I was hoisted into the bath and washed. More humiliation, but I just kept smiling and laughing, knowing one day I'd be doing all these things like shaving, arse wiping and bathing on my own. I'll tell you what, though, I didn't half feel refreshed after that bath; Deb was definitely pleased I'd had one.

Deb was really involved in all my rehab as I had hoped and wanted; after all, Deb would be my carer. One day she even came into hospital to see what might be expected of her when I did get home. Now the shaving Deb gave me I could handle, but the arse wiping was a little bit more embarrassing for both of us. Well, whatever; we got through it and hoped that by the time I could come home I'd be doing it myself (I was).

As my walking rehab on the frame was going well the physics moved me onto the next stage. Now this stage would involve me being without the walking frame for a few minutes because the next stage was doing stairs (shit). I say 'shit', but I thought in myself that I could do this, and anyway I needed to as me and Deb lived in a second-floor maisonette.

Well, now I could walk to the stairs with my walking frame, no wheelchair now; like I said I wasn't as nervous or apprehensive about the stairs as I was about the walking frame, and this was because even though my legs would be moving I knew that it would be my arms which would be taking most of my weight. Yeah, maybe not right but this was my first time and I had to adapt with my own safety of mind.

Well, I listened closely to the physic's instructions of right leg followed by left going down and opposite going up and, boom, it's there he's done it. Another feat achieved, another defeat for Him who tried to destroy me. It was only one stair, but that was enough for now. I would do more gradually to build me up for the real challenge of attempting – well, not attempting but *doing* – because if I wanted to go home, which obviously I did, I'd have to do two flights of stairs. Not trying to sound cocky, but I knew in myself that I could do them after that first stair in physio.

Once again my walking was progressing at a rate of knots and my arm was slowly but surely catching up. With my arm the OTs had moved me on to another stage of rehab, which was to get me in the staff kitchen and do the menial, simple task of making coffee and buttering some toast; sounds simple, yeah? Well no; for a start, I'm being watched over which makes most of us feel uneasy and I'm dealing with dangerous items like knives, a kettle full of boiling water and a dodgy left arm which I'm constantly being told by the OT to use at every opportunity. Oh, and let's not forget a brain that gets confused very easily (more later).

It must have taken me about half an hour to butter one slice of toast and make one cup of coffee, but no matter how long it took it was done and would get better and quicker so it was another triumph. Once again there were congratulations from Dot, Frank and Deb; yeah Dot, Frank and Deb, the three people who had probably been through the worst times of their lives with the stroke, two of which had no choice but to support me, (Dot, Frank) and one (Deb) who could have jumped ship and gone her own way but didn't. Deb stayed and supported me and wasn't going anywhere; oh no, she was seeing this out and staying for the whole performance.

I was in love with Deb before this happened and now seeing her stand by me like that with everything that had happened just made my love for her grow stronger, so in my mind it was inevitable the question I would ask Deb; yep, you've guessed it, I asked Deb to marry me. I had asked her this before in the dark days of my marriage to Him, but I think that when I asked her back then it wasn't really a one hundred per cent *me* asking; a large percentage of asking back then was down to Him.

Anyway, before asking I was a little bit nervous as to what the answer would be, but only a little bit 'cause you see for some reason I was ninety per cent sure that Deb would say yes, especially with all that had happened. I did say to Deb that she totally had to mean yes for both of us and

*Return Ticket Please*

that it wasn't just a sympathy yes, and she did mean it for us because you know what she said. She said if I hadn't asked she would've asked me. Wow, I was overwhelmed with a wave of happiness when she told me that.

Well, there we had it; what a year! A stroke, going to get married and in between all this we would eventually move. So me and Deb were going to marry. We now had to tell our happy news to everyone we knew; everyone was happy for us and I think the people who knew me best realised that for once in my life I had done something right and it was all done without Him. Even Dot was happy, I think. She didn't say much, but I think she was. I don't know why, but for some reason I got the impression that Dot didn't like Deb. Or maybe was it that now she knew everything that had happened with all my dark secrets coming out that, for the first time in my life I was ready; my time had come to finally grow up properly. Whatever it was, Dot is Dot and even though I never tell her, I do love her dearly.

With all the good news there was more and more determination inside me, but there was one slight problem; you see one of the staff nurses was a little concerned that I was becoming a bit too hospitalised, which I was. Things were going great in physio – my walking was improving, my left arm was doing more – so with Easter just round the corner she told me and Deb over the Easter holidays, 'Scram, get out of my sight, I don't want to see you two over the holidays.' Excellent. Do you know if you've been in hospital for a while what it's like to hear them words? Well orgasmic, bloody orgasmic. So here it was; Easter and me and Deb had four days' leave from the hospital.

*Derek Williams*

Four days' leave, man! I couldn't wait for Deb to come and pick me up from the hospital. Inside I was a little child at Christmas. I got dressed as well as I could at this stage – you see I was still mainly being dressed by the nurses. I could just about get my boxers and trousers on, even though it took me about fifteen minutes; socks and shoes were a bit more of a problem so I had to be aided but the biggest problem of all was my top. Jesus Christ, I don't know how many times the nurses had shown me the right way to put a top on, but I just couldn't get the hang of it. This will probably sound silly, but to put a top on all I had to do was stick my left arm in the left arm sleeve first of all and then follow with the right arm into the right sleeve and the rest followed, but could I do it? Could I hell. You see, my brain was telling me to do it the other way; you know, right arm first the way we have done it for years. Well, no matter how many times I was shown or had it explained to me it just wasn't happening, that is until the first day of mine and Deb's Easter break and Deb explained it to me. When Deb came to pick me up I was dressed apart from a top. Enter Deb and help me. She did help me, she explained it to me in more or less the same way as the nurses had, but for some reason it just seemed to sink in my head better when explained by Deb. I'm not saying I could put my top on straight away with ease, but I now understood the basics and from the basics I would progress to putting my top on alone. Well, I was ready except for one final – and to me very important – touch: the hair. Oh yeah, I'm a gel man and this was as important to me as putting my trousers on. What I didn't know at the time, because I don't think Deb had the heart to tell me, was that

*Return Ticket Please*

I was in fact putting shaving gel in my hair; well whatever, I was now finally ready.

This first day out was going to be exciting for both of us no matter what we did, although I do think it was a little bit nerve-racking for Deb as she had to control the wheelchair. Now this is a job I certainly wouldn't like to do, especially when having to manoeuvre it onto a bus. Now this is probably a job that experienced wheelchair users don't enjoy, so for a first-timer like Deb it must have been pretty nerve-racking. However, she felt she did brilliantly and made it look like she'd been doing it for years. Well, we got into town and I'll tell you what's amazing: how much you appreciate something or somewhere you haven't been or seen for a month. It was great to be out of hospital. This was something I thought I wasn't going to do in a very long time; what were we going to do with our freedom? I didn't care; I just wanted to enjoy each other's company out of hospital grounds. Deb was doing great with the wheelchair, pushing me through town like a professional. The only problem she encountered with the wheelchair was with the smaller kerbs; they were a bit of a nuisance and on a few occasions I almost came flying out of the chair. (Minor problem.)

Literally about fifteen minutes into our day out we bumped into a very good friend of mine, Vincenzo. I've known Vince for about ten years; I worked with him at Don Giovanni's and La Gondola. Vince had had a drug problem a few years before this happened to me and I'd helped him out by talking to him and listening very closely to his problem and generally giving him some good advice, which he listened to. Of course the advice I was giving to Vince was good because unbeknown to him I was suffering the same problem: an addiction. OK, mine wasn't cocaine like Vince's, mine was alcohol, but weigh them both up and which is worse? Of course I'll say alcohol but others will say cocaine, but remember they are both hard drugs because of the addiction. One is cheaper and legal, one is bought just like that from thousands of pubs, clubs, off-licences and so on, and one almost cost me my life! When Vince had told me about his problem I admired him for having the courage to tell me – well, not just me; everybody that Vince knew also knew about his problem, and soon everybody that I knew would also know my problem. Anyway, this was a nice start to our day out to bump into a good friend. The only reason Vince never visited me in hospital was simply because he didn't know what had happened, unlike some of my other so-called mates, who I'll come to later who did know what had happened but didn't bother (tossers).

Me and Deb walked around town and decided we'd go and feed the ducks in Elizabeth Gardens (old haunt); feed the ducks, no way in a million years would you see or even hear of me feeding ducks before the stroke, and in Elizabeth Gardens! Surely not. I mean, before the stroke Elizabeth Gardens had been used as one of my various private bars. Well, this was a new me, a sober me, a me away from Him, and if I wanted to feed ducks and be more boring than before then I was going to. I'd done my share of hell-raising; I'd finished my relationship with Him, I was now on the straight and narrow. Well, we went down there armed with our loaf of Tesco's cheapest to be confronted by no ducks; oh well, not to worry, there'll be other times.

Duck operation over and unsuccessful, me and Deb decided to go for some lunch in the Chicago Rock. Here we have it: my first entry into one of His many homes. How would I cope? Would I succumb to the temptations of His awesome powers? I mean, did He still have some sort of hold over me? Of course not, surely He didn't think I was going to be one of His disciples again – or did He? Let's not forget He can be very persuasive, and after all, did anybody really think that on my first day out I was going to enjoy His pleasures and especially in the company of Deb and having to be returned to the hospital at some point? No, I was very happy just to be sat there with Deb and my mineral water. But as I said, this was just my first day out, there was excitement in me; I mean, what would or will happen if that excitement dies? Well, this is something that hasn't and I hope will never happen, I say 'hopefully' because you never know; He's got me before, although to get me again He'd have to try bloody hard! This will always be a constant worry to Deb and others who care about me, but it's harder on Deb as she sees me from day to day. But Deb is very good because she's not a big drinker and very seldom is there the temptation of Him in our flat.

Back to our day out. I said earlier in the book that just before the stroke happened me and Deb were getting a bit fruity and that was all the sex that you were getting in this book; that wasn't true because as me and Deb were sitting there eating our lunch the subject of sex cropped up. Now I said earlier that I'd been a bit worried because my weapon hadn't been showing much life down there, it hadn't been twinging at all, but it had started to wake up and believe me, now with me and Deb sitting down eating our lunch and talking about sex he was definitely awake. Oh yes, he was most certainly twinging. It had been weeks, days, hours, minutes, seconds since the last time me and Deb had had sex, and let me put it plainly: we were both gagging for it. Now I may have put that in a crude way, but I'm sorry it's how we both felt. You may be thinking, 'Sex! You're in a wheelchair in a pub; you've got no chance!' Well, you're wrong, because it's amazing what you can achieve when you want something as badly as we did. I won't go through the whole show, just the basics.

As I'm disabled we purchased a key that could open any disabled toilet in town; just so happens the Chicago Rock has one, then Deb manoeuvred me into the toilet and got in herself. There's not much room in these toilets but there was enough for what we were planning to do. Let me cut to the chase; it's sufficient to say that after the foreplay everything was pretty much up to Deb as I was unable to move properly. Like I said, I'm only giving you the basics, the rest you can work out for yourselves, but I will just say this: it was the best orgasm I'd ever had.

Anyway, now we had had sex, made love – call it what you want – we were both really happy as it had been a bit worrying if we'd be able to make love again. So what do most people do if they try something out and they really enjoy it? They do it again: me and Deb are no different. We made love in BHS, Maltings Toilet, Hospital Toilet, again in Chicago Rock. Christ, we even got well fruity on my bed in the hospital – behind closed curtains, of course. So there we had it: mine and Deb's four days out over the Easter period involved wandering round town, having lunch in pubs and lovemaking. Excellent.

This little Easter break for me and Deb was really exciting. Yeah, I never thought I'd say it, but just walking around town and really not doing much (lovemaking excluded) was exciting. Christ, before the stroke happened the only reason I'd go into town would be to pick Him up from the pub or off-licence and enjoy only His company, but now here I was totally sober and enjoying myself without Him. Trouble was (and still is) will these normal everyday things keep me excited? We shall see!

Well, mine and Deb's little holiday was drawing to a close and it was going to be time to go back to my new home, the hospital but rather than being all down and depressed I was excited. Yeah, I was champing at the bit to continue my physio. You see, I'd had a taste of freedom and now I wanted to finish my meal; I now knew the finishing line was close, yeah very close. In fact, it was so close that now there was talk of me coming home.

Coming home, blimey! Even though I knew it was going to happen some time it was now there right in front of me! The physics had done their work and they were happy with me; Dr Walters, my consultant, was happy with me; I was happy with me; Deb was happy with me. Christ, everyone was happy, so let's get the wheels in motion!

*CHAPTER*
## Eleven

NOW, WHEN coming home from such a long stay in hospital and having had a stroke its not a case of, 'Well, that's it, Derek, we've done our bit your on your own now.' Oh no, there are procedures to follow, channels to go down because after all I've had a stroke; my whole life has changed, Deb's life has changed; so even though there was the talk of me coming home we still knew it was a little way away and in our case it was a little further away because we lived in a second-floor maisonette.

Firstly there was a meeting with Dr Walters. I wasn't actually in on this meeting but Deb and Dot were. I think the reason for me not being in on the meeting was simply 'cause it was nothing to do with me; I think it was more of a meeting for the people who would be caring for and seeing me the most; you know a separate meeting for the people who were closest to me. It was a chance for them to ask their questions of what to expect, what do we do if such and such happens or basically put, how much better would I get (no answer to that). As Deb once said to me, 'Dot is how a lot of us would wish to be.' By this she meant Dot is very good at asking questions and very good at getting answers explained in an understandable way, whereas Deb, and she has said this countless times to me, isn't. Nothing wrong with that; eighty-five per cent of the population is probably like that. This meeting was also definitely good for Dot, because I think she was feeling a bit left out. I know for sure that she thought things were being kept from her; why she thought this I don't know, but she had got this into her head a long time ago, even down in Southampton, and it's because of this I think she was funny towards Deb. I can, hand on heart, say nothing was kept from Dot and if something was to be kept from Dot it would have been my decision to keep it away from her and not Deb's. Well, I think after this meeting Dot was far happier, I think she got a lot of questions off her chest; whether she listened to the answers I'll never know. Also in this meeting there was the important talk of the plan that would be drawn up to continue my physio and occupational therapy once I was back home. Oh yeah, just because I was to be back home and out of hospital it didn't mean that was it. God no, I still had months and months of physio and OT to come (more later). Deb told me that at this part of the meeting she quite abruptly told Dot that she'd need her help (brave Deb) all because she was making out that we'd never need her help; God why were you like this, Dot?

In addition to this meeting there was to be another one involving Deb, my head physio, my social worker and myself. In this meeting we discussed where me and Deb lived and what adjustments would have to be made to the maisonette, adjustments such as banisters on our stairs, grab rails in our toilet and bathroom, a raised toilet seat and raisers on our sofas. This would all be done through the hospital. Also discussed at the meeting was the all-important subject of how would I be able to cope with getting up and down two flights of stairs? Or more to the point, would I be able to at all? Well, inside myself I was quietly confident that it would be no problem, providing Deb was there to keep an eye on me. Anyway, I had to make sure I could do the stairs because the other alternative was for me to basically be housebound until the council could move us to a ground-floor place, which could take months!

The talk had been done about the concerns of the stairs so the next step was to put talk into practise; yeah it was decided that the head physio and head OT would take me to my home and see how I would cope with the stairs and also see how I would generally cope around the house now that all the adjustments had been made. The only problem was, they were going to take me home for a few hours and then bring me back to hospital. Oh well, never mind, it's a step closer to getting back home proper.

We reached my home with walking frame in tow; yep had to bring my old buddy, the walking frame, but like I said, I was quietly confident about doing the stairs as was I quietly confident about not needing the walking frame. As I'd done a little – and I do mean a little – bit of walking without it at the hospital, I had decided I would walk from the car to the stairs without it, obviously with my two guards by my side. Well, we pulled up and Deb was waiting outside and I did it: I walked without the frame to the entrance of our block, yeah a short distance to anyone else, but a marathon to me. I think I shocked my physio, OT and Deb. Deb texted me later to say how proud she was of me, this text made me really proud as well and was sweet.

Now, with this part of my journey done it was to the stairs. There they were and in my confident mood I climbed up them carefully and in my own time; speed wasn't the test here, assurance was. Going up has always been easier to me, I've achieved that and as the saying goes, what goes up must come down, and I did. I came down safely and much slower than going up – yeah, definitely much slower; after all, I was looking to come out of hospital, not spend more time in there with a broken leg. I'd done it; the stairs were done. The next part was to go back up to our home and see how I coped around the house, so firstly I had to go up our stairs to the toilet, test out grab rails, toilet seat and so on, and come back down the stairs, this time with Deb watching me. After all, it wasn't me just on trial; Deb was as well; she had to be because she was going to be doing an awful lot of watching me go up and come down stairs.

Things were going superbly and got even better when I showed great calm and awareness in doing my last task, which was to make us all a cuppa. Sounds easy? Try it in my state. Anyway, in achieving this I had shown that I could be safe in the kitchen doing the basics, more would come later. So that was it; everything had been a success. It was agreed that it was safe for me to come back home (excellent). Bit of a shame I had to go back to the hospital, but I was closer to coming home and was as excited as I'd ever been. I'll give you a clue on my excitement. That day after all the walking I'd done I was knackered and should have zonked out straight away, but the excitement and adrenalin were keeping me awake. The adrenalin and excitement were going to keep me going for the next week, because even though I'd had the go-ahead to go home there was still the little inconvenience of the hospital having to dot the 'i's and cross the 't's (you know what I mean) but hey, this was no problem considering a few weeks before I thought I'd still be in there at Christmas time. I was also happy with the fact I'd be home to see Southampton in the FA Cup Final (poor showing).

The 'i's had been dotted and the 't's had been crossed, and I was told by the staff nurse I'd be leaving hospital on Friday. Friday – bloody hell that's only like two days away! Well, I can tell you my excitement had reached fever point, but also mixed in with my excitement was a great deal of apprehension, worry and nervousness, because let's not forget I would now be stepping into the unknown, there would be no Him. Of course I tried to express to Deb, who was also excited, my worries, but you see I'm one of these people who can express my feelings without ever really expressing them, if you know what I mean. In other words, I talk about how I feel but I never really get to the core of how I feel, I just give you the outer coating.

Well anyway, with this talked about I think I'd got out how I felt but in my own way. However, I felt my worrying feelings certainly weren't going to overshadow my feelings of excitement. I had a day to go and I was out – or was I? Because you see, the staff nurse had made a mistake. I wasn't coming out on the Friday. Oh no, I was informed by my OT I was being released on the Monday. Why? Well, the reason for this was they had no transport (bloody hell). In the weeks, months I'd been in hospital I'd never really let my spirits get down but now having had my dream whisked away from me just like that, I was down; not just me, Deb was too. Now you may think, 'Oh come on, it's only another two days!' Well, having been in hospital for so long, two days is like a millennium. Well anyway one day dragged past and then the second day clawed its way to an end and then *Boom!* we're there its here *Monday*, Monday, the day me and Deb have been waiting for. Fling open the doors and let me out: I'm ready. Yeah one problem: I may have been ready but the hospital wasn't because I had to wait for Dr Walters to come round and check on me one last time – you know, explain about medication, wish me good luck, say his goodbyes (ah, bless!) and warn me about the dangers of binge drinking. You see, the hospital still thought the stroke was caused by binge drinking. I thought they knew I was an alcoholic so when Dr Walters said to me, 'You can still drink but in moderation,' it set off alarm bells in Deb's head. Me and Deb talked about the prospects of Him coming back into my life after being given the all-clear by the doctor, that I could drink again and I think I managed to silence the bells, but only silenced them because they'll never go off in Deb's head.

# CHAPTER
# Twelve

WELL, IT WAS almost upon us; the time to leave my temporary home was just hours away; of course there were thoughts running through my head of, *Could I, could I really go into the outside world and survive, could I cope without Him?* Well in my own mind I confidently thought, *Yes, yes of course I can*, and do you know why I was so confident? I was so confident because of that word 'challenge'. Yes, now coming out of hospital into the outside world with my physical and mental disabilities everything was going to be a challenge, but these challenges weren't going to be like the ones I'd had when I was with Him and he'd aid me through them, oh no these were *my* challenges there was to be no Him, ever.

Well, with the clock ticking away me and Deb were anxiously waiting for Dr Walters to come round and give the OK, but before he came round I had another task to do – not so much a task but a question to ask him. Yes, a question, a very simple question, but it was one of those questions I had to build up a bit of courage for because, yes, of course this question was about sex. I s'pose the majority of us get a little bit embarrassed about asking a question on this subject; I certainly did. You see, Deb had been saying to me about this and was going on about asking a nurse. I thought, *Ask a nurse, you must be joking! I'm asking the main man, Dr Walters.* I never told Deb that I was going to ask him, so I think she was a little surprised when I did. All the question was, simply: would it be safe to have sex? The answer was a goodish one; it was a yes but it would probably be better to wait till after my angiogram. *What?* My angiogram was about a month away, no way could me and Deb hold out that long – could we? No, if I was to be back home we wanted to make love in the comfort of our bed and not the toilets of BHS, so we did and it was great.

Well, it was so close. Dr Walters had visited me for the last time; my transport had been booked; I was there. My time had been completed. My transport arrived a couple of hours after Dr Walters had gone (excruciating wait). I said goodbye to the nurses who had been *brilliant* and was wheeled away to my carriage to be driven home and start a life, a new life without Him (scary). Even though I was back home now, the hospital was still going to be my second home, I still had loads of physio, occupational therapy and tests to do and one of these tests was my angiogram.

What's an angiogram? Basically an angiogram is where they give you a local anaesthetic in the groin area and flush a dye round inside your body to check for any more blood clots. I was pretty confident they wouldn't find any more as the clot I'd had in the first place had been caused by Him and He hadn't been seen for weeks. It's amazing that what He had done to me was now making me produce my own strength and courage to do things I'd never have done without Him inside me first. I mean, do you really think I'd have had something like an angiogram done in the old days without Him? No chance; yeah, you may be thinking, There's no way you could have gone in the hospital in the old days with Him inside you! Forget it, done it because don't forget in them days nothing would part me from Him.

Well, as it was, the angiogram was all clear so now it was back to my new life without Him, who was now becoming a distant memory, but not too distant because since I'd been out of hospital He'd been nowhere to be seen; how would I cope when His ugly mug did appear around me? Well, as I've said, Deb isn't a massive drinker and had in fact said that she'd give up drinking all together if I wanted her to (cheers, babe) but I said no, 'cause this was something I'd have to get used to, other people drinking around me; I mean, I can't expect the whole world to give up drinking just because of me. I will say this: I've a small group of people who are still in contact with me since this has happened (more later) and they always ask if I mind them drinking around me which to me shows respect.

But anyway, how would I cope when the first test of Him entering into my life again, Him being near me, in the same room as me? I couldn't avoid the situation for ever, could I? So mine and His first encounter was to come on my home ground, yeah bring it on. Deb's mates, Mandy and Sarah, were coming down to ours for the three of them to enjoy a bottle of wine, which I was fine about; I was forcing it into me that this Devil juice was theirs not mine; them days have gone. Well, Deb would ask me if I was still OK with the whole thing and I'd say, 'Yeah, course I am babe,' which I can wholeheartedly say I was. I mean, after all, it was just going to be three people sitting down drinking my old best buddy, wasn't it?

Mandy and Sarah came down, Mandy even bought me a

bottle of that non-alcoholic wine, which is actually quite nice. I'd forced it into myself that this was only going to last for a couple of hours, mine and His first meeting, and after that couple of hours everything would just be back to normal, which it was. It was done. Our first encounter was over and I'd come out on top, but this was only our first encounter there'd be more (as there still will be); how would I cope with them?

I'll tell you what, though, it's amazing being around people when you're sober, you know, seeing how they go through the phases of soberness to light-headedness and then drunk, not blind in your face fall over drunk, but just pleasantly drunk, and I'll say another thing, God, don't they go on? You ask them the most simple of questions and Christ won't they *murder* the answer. My God, I must have been talking the biggest load of garbage for years!

Anyway, I'll come back to other encounters with Him a bit later. For now, I'd just like to tell you about the new regime of physio and occupational therapy that would soon be confronting me. As I've said, the hospital would be my second home, eventually; I say eventually because there was a bit of a wait from me coming home until the hospital contacted me about continuing my programme. I don't know why, but my GP, Dr Newton Dunn, wasn't too impressed as we had to get me back to being totally independent. Well, he phoned the hospital and must have used his clout and called in a few favours, because within a couple of days the hospital was in contact and asking me to go up there for a bit of an introduction with a bit of walking thrown in; you know, a 'let's see what we got to work with' exercise.

On the way up to the hospital Deb asked me if I was nervous, and yeah, I must admit I was, because this was something new; I'd be working with and meeting new people. If that had happened in the olden days, He'd be there to hold my hand through the whole experience; now it was just me.

All my physio and OT was on Nunton Ward, and on getting there I was still nervous. We had a little wait; me, Deb, and of course my walking frame, before Sam, the head of the department, came over, introduced herself and asked me to follow her. More or less the first thing she said was, 'We'll have you off that walking frame by the end of the session!' I thought, *Yeah right.*

The session involved Sam explaining what would be involved in the programme and also a few questions about myself, one of the questions being what caused my stroke to which I answered, 'Too much of the good life.' I assumed once again that Sam would know what I meant by that answer; I honestly thought she knew I meant I was an alcoholic, but no; I would find out later that all the staff I would come to work with thought my stroke was caused by binge drinking! This would all come out later that, yeah, the stroke was caused by drink, but also that I was an alcoholic.

Anyway, with my programme explained to me, Sam wanted to see me walk a bit; obviously this physio I was doing now was a bit more advanced than what I'd been doing at Farley. Although to me I thought I was walking pretty good – yeah, stumbling and desperately trying to keep my balance – I was in fact walking pretty bad because basically all my weight was going through my right side, even when I stood up all my weight was on my right side; you see, my brain was taking the safe option. Nevertheless, this was all going to be worked on; they would try and get my weight balanced evenly.

Anyway, before my session had ended Sam introduced me to my next walking buddy; oh yes, I was introduced to my crutch. I say my buddy because I quite immaturely gave my crutch a name. I thought, *Yeah, why not?* After all, he was going to be the one aiding me to walk, he was going to be the one stopping me from falling flat on my face, wasn't he? Anyway, I named him Chipper, I think to the disgust of Deb. It was a stupid thing to do but I'll tell you what, old Chipper is still mentioned today occasionally by me, Dez and Ben.

I took well to Chipper and it was another step to my target of being able to walk independently; he gave me and Deb more independence and also gave Deb a well-earned rest, as our previous ventures into town had involved Deb pushing me around in the wheelchair. Mind you, though, our first trip into town was quite amusing. I was walking round like some drunk; I think it took all of Chipper's strength to stop me from falling. In these early days I would get confused very easily (still do) and believe me, if you had the easy way to walk or the awkward way, yeah, you guessed it I'd take the awkward way much to my and Deb's amusement. God it was hilarious, as were a few other things that happened, like the time I woke up and quite wimpily said to Deb, 'Babe, I'm stuck in the duvet!' Yeah, don't ask me how, but somehow I'd managed to get myself wrapped up in the duvet and because of the confusion that had set in my brain, Deb had to unravel me!

All this confusion that was happening in my brain was another effect of the stroke. As I've said, certain parts of my brain had been killed off so I would find very simple tasks more confusing and difficult, but this would be worked on up the hospital by the OTs in cognitive thinking sessions. The reason for these sessions is to try and make new pathways for the electrical currents in your brain. The majority of these sessions would be held with the head OT, Jo Gibson, who I think is brilliant at her job, and the sessions involved things like looking at a map and circling hotels, YHS, railway stations and so on. It also involved listening exercises where I'd have to listen to an audio tape of someone droning on (bit like me) and listen out for beeps over the top of his voice. Then I moved on to the map circling and listening exercises together. May sound boring to you, but to me it was a *must* and also it was keeping me busy, which meant my mind wasn't on Him. Out of the two exercises of visual and listening I was definitely better at the listening ones; my visual to brain coordination wasn't very good, in fact it was appalling, as was proved on one exercise I had to do.

All this exercise involved was putting a jigsaw of a body together. There were two arms, two legs, a body and a head – oh, and hands, feet and so on. In all there were ten pieces and the pieces weren't small, I mean they were about fifteen centimetres big. There was a time limit of five minutes on this task and I confidently thought to myself, *Five minutes? No problem. What am I supposed to do with the other four minutes thirty seconds?* if you know what I mean. Well, the pieces were then scattered around on the table. All I was waiting for was the starter's gun, then there it went; Jo gave me the nod to begin. Begin? Begin what? I was a blank, my brain was going in all sorts of directions but not the right one. I thought to myself, *What the f\*\*k is happening here? I'm struggling here, well not really struggling more like I can't do this.* Yeah, I got the body and head no probs, but come to the arms and legs I was flummoxed. I couldn't see or understand how they joined onto the body. With a minute left Jo asked if I wanted to stop, but like a typical Taurus (stubborn). I said, 'No,' so I saw out that last minute trying to put a two-year-old's jigsaw together and failing miserably. I couldn't believe what had just happened. Well, at least being in the hospital and not out in public you know you're not going to be laughed at for this horrendous effort at such an easy task, so Jo sat with me and went over how to put the jigsaw together, and with her help it now looked so simple.

Now we had done a few tests we had pinpointed the weaker areas of my brain, so now we could do more tests on them, so as to open the pathways for my electrical currents to find different routes to their destination. I would be given a variety of tests to do at home, which I really enjoyed doing and have helped. I won't bore you to death (if I haven't already) with all the tests I did at home, I'll just leave it with the jigsaw test because it's always been the most prominent in my mind, and hopefully will give you an idea of what state of confusion my brain was in. Believe me, it was in confusion; it would be a while until I could go anywhere on my own.

With every session of physio and occupational therapy I was having I was becoming more and more aware that I did have a left side as well as a right; I was starting to even my body out bit by bit. My balance and centre of gravity was getting there – not totally right (still isn't), but progress was being made. I was even starting to involve my left arm more, though I didn't have much choice in that one, because every time my right hand went to pick up something I was told straight away, 'Use your left arm, Derek.' You see, it was getting drummed into my brain to use it, bit like training a dog to sit I s'pose.

I was be going up the hospital at least three times a week for my physio and OT sessions. Now some people might find that well tedious and have the attitude of, 'Oh God not physio again,' but I actually enjoyed it. To me the sessions were a great laugh. I remember Sam saying to me once in one particularly hilarious session that, 'This is physio, you're not supposed to be enjoying it.' Well, I'm sorry, Sam, but I *was* enjoying it and just couldn't control my non-stop laughter from start to finish.

My physio and OT were falling nicely into place, my walking was improving, my left arm was starting to function; but these are the things people can see, they can't see or understand why you get confused so much or why your reactions are slower than they used to be. Basically they can't see your brain; yeah neither could I but I knew what was going on in it and of course who was public enemy number one in my brain; yeah, of course it was Him.

Him, Him, Him, my good old buddy from the past, a friend that will always rear His head up from time to time in my life. You may think, 'But Derek, you've faced Him already and defeated Him.' Yeah, I have, haven't I? But that was just the battle, the war will go on for ever, won't it?

My next battle with Him would come on His home ground and it would take place in the Chicago Rock. Previous to this encounter Deb had been out a couple of weeks beforehand and I remember saying to her, 'Do you think we'll be able to go out together like we did before, minus Him of course?' And she said, 'Yeah, of course we will.' She said, 'In fact, there's a Meatloaf impersonator down the Rock in a couple of weeks; we'll go to that if you want.' I was up for that straight away, but it was a couple of weeks away; how would I feel as the time got closer? Would His words of, 'Come on, Derek, this is our chance to be reunited,' make me crack?

Well, I must admit that on the day of the Meatloaf gig I was in two minds as to whether I was going to go or not. The reason I was pondering as to whether I was going was of course firstly because of Him, but also because I'd be sober and I must admit that scared me. I was scared because the people around me would obviously be drinking and we all know that when people drink they loosen up, they get silly. Well, tonight that wouldn't be happening to me; tonight for the first time a lot of people would be seeing me out for a night as me – and not me and Him, I mean. What would people think of me? What would *I* think of me? Would we see that young man who needed His help in any scary, nervous situation? Or would we see the old Derek who'd be brimming with confidence with His help? OK I might have passed the first test of people drinking around me when Deb's friends came around, but that was just three people, now it was going to be a whole pub full. Also, on top of this it would be my first time in a really packed place with Chipper; how would I cope with that? Would I get pushed over? What about going to the toilet? Would there be a seat for me to sit on? Well, I can tell you my mind was a muddle with all these unanswered questions. Anyway, on the bus down a calm came upon me as I drew strength from what had actually happened to me. I mean, I'd been through a hell of a lot, hadn't I? Surely I could handle one night out, I mean it was *one* night out. Yeah, admittedly I'd be sober, which was unheard of for me, but so what? That's nothing compared to having to re-teach your body to function again, is it?

Well, on getting to the Rock I felt confident and comfortable in myself and my confidence was boosted as I saw all my mates were there: there was me, Deb, Alan, Tina, Dez, Paul, Rosie, little Mark, Sarah. They all gave me their congratulations and asked questions, as you'd expect, but that wasn't the main thing on my mind or probably not your minds; of course the main issue here was what would I have to drink? Well, I know I've written all this stuff about Him and how He'd tried to destroy me, but upon reaching the Rock, who did two drinks for the price of one, I'd decided that my first drink was going to be half a pint of lager. Yeah, you may be thinking, 'Half a pint of lager? That's Him, that's alcohol – why have you bothered to tell us all this shit if at the first opportunity you get you're just going back to Him?' Well, that is a very good point, but you must understand I did that for me, not Him. You see, firstly I actually wanted to enjoy a taste of His blood for the enjoyment of it and not for the necessity of it, and secondly I wanted to prove to myself that I could drink Him and be in control of Him and not Him being the one in control; a risky test maybe, but I had to be the one who silenced His voice in my head. Yeah, I'm not going to silence them totally on half a pint of lager and may never, but for my own peace of mind and Deb's it was a start. Judge it as you want, but it was my mind He'd been f\*\*\*ing with all them years, so this was my decision, nobody else's, and after all, with what I'd been through because of Him do you really think I was going to let Him rule my life again? OK, after the fits I'd had He'd weaselled His way back into my life but not this time, no way. Anyway, I must admit I enjoyed that lager and there's the difference between years back and now; I enjoyed it for the drink it was and not for the addiction it had become years ago.

The night was turning out to be really enjoyable. I was having a new experience, I was sober and having a good time; years ago I'd never thought that possible! On my next drink I toned down; I had a shandy. Now this concerned Deb. Why? Well, the reason for that is that Deb associates shandy as being an alcoholic drink. Personally, I don't. Make your own minds up about that one.

As I've said, the night was really good and it was to get better as my mate, Alan, had asked the DJ to put one of my favourite Queen songs on ('Don't Stop Me Now'). Well, that was it, I lost all inhibitions of my condition and got on the packed dance floor with Deb, Al, Tina and Dez and had a boogie. Of course when I say boogie we weren't talking John Travolta *Saturday Night Fever*; no, we were more like talking 'feet firmly on floor, hold onto banister and move body slightly' fever. Well, whatever it was or however it looked, in my book it was boogying and I think I surprised myself and the others around me. I know for sure Alan was surprised because Alan, who to be truthful is quite an emotional chap, was stood there gobsmacked and on the brink of crying (calm down, Al, don't make a show of yourself). I think the reason for Alan's show of emotion is that he saw me the day the stroke had happened. He was there when I was going through the fit motion of the stroke and it was Al who took Deb to Southampton that day.

What a great night that was, and despite having that early lager and shandy, for the rest of the night I had mineral water.

# CHAPTER
# Thirteen

ANOTHER THING happened that night between me and Him, and this is something I'm revealing for the first time. You see, He's crafty, He'd try anything to get back with me. He knew all too well that I wasn't going to be out all night drinking Him in front of Deb and my mates, so He passed it into my brain to do a bit of minesweeping when there was nobody around. 'Yeah right, good try, but no thanks this isn't the old Derek.' But you see, that's what He's like, He'll keep trying and trying until He gets what He wants. Yeah, in the old days He'd have gotten what He wanted, but old Friend, these ain't the old days.

As the night came to an end I was knackered. I'd had a great night and I'd beaten Him in another round of our fight, I'd passed the test of going out with a group of people who'd be pissed when I'd be sober. I must say, though, for some reason I felt more comfortable with the larger number of people who were drinking rather than that night when it was just Deb, Mandy and Sarah.

Now that I'd been out for a night and had a smidgen of His blood, how would I be the next morning? Because let's not forget that in the days of mine and His friendship He'd be with me or not far away from me throughout the whole day, and that included days me and Deb had off together. On those days when we woke up together my first job of the day would be to nip into the toilet and pick Him up from behind the toilet cistern or whip Him out from my trouser pocket where He'd been enjoying a good night's sleep. Whichever it was, He'd be guzzled down in the privacy of the toilet (in seconds) then crushed, put back in my pocket and discarded when I went to the shop to stock up on His life-giving blood.

Anyway, on this morning there was no such repeat of the olden days; if He was calling me I wasn't hearing, or maybe just not listening! I'll say something, though, when I did wake up that morning I had a little bit of a headache. Wow, you may say. Yeah, I agree it probably is something very minor to you, but to me it was quite significant as in the olden days I'd never woken up with any kind of a headache no matter how much I'd been partying with Him. I was happy with what I'd achieved that night, I was happy with how the physical side was improving,; things were looking up until I had another knock back. Even though He wasn't in my life any more I got a reminder of the damage He'd done to me.

Everything bad that has happened to me in my adult life has all been down to Him, and this next bad and to be honest very scary experience was no different. I'd been feeling funny for a couple of days on and off. Best way to explain it is that I was having the anxiety attacks I'd experienced before when I'd fitted. Now I didn't really think that much about the feelings and never said anything to Deb until it was too late, and then no explaining had to be done because it was there right in front of her. I'll never forget. I was sat on the bed and the anxiety feelings had reached a level too far; it was then I said to Deb but within seconds,

*Boom!* there were flashing lights and it felt like I was foaming at the mouth. Obviously with this happening there was a panic in the bedroom. I was still conscious and remember Deb, who was also in a state of panic, phoning for an ambulance and even though in a state of panic quite superbly putting me in the recovery position. I could still talk, even though my mouth drooped to the left, and I said to David to get Dez who lived just across the road and is very good in these situations and who I knew would be good support for Deb. What was happening? Deb was thinking the worst, thinking I was having another stroke. Myself, I didn't think I was because this didn't feel the same as the stroke; there was no massive explosion in my head like with the stroke. Anyway, I can remember the ambulance people getting there and then nothing; I lost consciousness. What was happening? Well, I was having a fit. I had another one in the ambulance on the way to the hospital. So why was I fitting? Basically due to the stroke and the brain surgery I'd been left with scarring on the brain. Now for some reason, probably my thickness, it never occurred to me I was having a fit. I mean, I was on medication for fits. My consultant had told me there was a possibility of fitting but I couldn't remember that; but anyway there we have it, due to my years of hanging around with Him I am now epileptic. After that first fit I have since had about eight, after one of which I spent another night in hospital. My medication for my epilepsy has been shuffled around a bit to control it better and currently I'm on (boring) 400 mg phenytoin (morning) 400 mg Neurontin (morning, afternoon and night) 150 mg lamotrogine (morning and night). So in a way, every part of the day I'm reminded of the damage He's done to me.

I might be getting reminders of His cruelty to me, but like I've said the tide is turning in my favour, although there have been and still will be days when I hear His voices, and a couple of examples of these are when once Deb had accidentally left an open bottle of wine in the kitchen. Now this was His prime opportunity to try and get me back into His life. I could hear His voice trying to persuade me to take one glug of Him, just one glug, you know, just like the old days. I must admit the temptation was there, but I knew that even just one glug of Him in secret would be a massive risk and a huge backwards step. Yeah, I know I'd already joined up with Him on that night out, but Deb was there, I wasn't being sneaky about joining Him. If I'd taken that one glug He'd have won a round in our fight. I'd be doing what He asked of me, just like the old days. In addition to this, if I'd taken a sneaky glug I'd be deceiving Deb and I wasn't going to do that for anyone, no way. So as it was I did the right thing I ignored His voice and told Deb about the bottle of wine. Now Deb has always said to me that she doesn't understand what being an alcoholic is all about – who does if you haven't been there? So when I told her about my ex-Friend being within striking distance of me I think she took it the wrong way as she chucked Him down the sink quite stroppily. I'm not sure if she was annoyed at me or herself for leaving Him so close to me unattended. Whichever it was He was gone and out of my sight (for now).

If Deb was annoyed at me then, I'm sorry babe, but I had to say something because I was still in a fragile condition after mine and His divorce. You see, it's very hard for Deb not understanding alcoholism, it's a new experience for her and not a nice one. I mean, if I had the choice of being the alcoholic or being the one who loves the alcoholic and worries whether the alcoholic will be buying alcohol when he or she is up the shop or in town on their own I know whose shoes I'd rather be in; the alcoholic's. Of course, there were other times that I've been alone with Him (more later) but this was the first time since our split, so it was a poignant time in my recovery.

Moving away from that for a bit, these were busy times for me and Deb – well, mainly Deb – because there was a house move coming up, and of course there was our wedding to organise. In between all this we were invited to Paul and Rosie's wedding but that's not the main issue I want to talk about here. The main issue here is Paul's stag night. Yeah, I did pay Him another visit but I was controlled and stuck to my pint of lager and pint of shandy, which I was proud of because there was no Deb around and frankly I could have gone off the rails being let loose on my own in the pub environment that used to be my second home.

Anyway, it was on this night that I bumped into those so-called mates who I used to live with, you know the tossers who'd never bothered once to visit me in hospital. Here we had a case of 'you know who your mates are when you're in hospital'. Simply put, in my eyes they were no longer my mates.

As I walked into the pub, within seconds Richy came rushing over to me shouting, 'Del mate!'

Well, before he had a chance to say anything else I just said, 'Sorry ain't got time to talk,' and walked past him. My opportunity to explain my abruptness would come later.

Next it was the turn of Craig, who wandered up behind me outside looking quite nervous and said, 'All right, mate?' to which I replied, 'You didn't want to know me when I was in hospital so don't f***ing come round me now and expect me to want to know you.' Of course, word of this got around and minutes later I had Ian, a friend of theirs, and someone who I did know before my stroke coming over to me and saying, 'Come on, Del, don't be like that; they were concerned when you were in hospital, they'd ask Dez how you were when they saw him.'

Wow, big f***ing deal! I had people who I never really knew but Dot did asking her how I was, and anyway, if you're that concerned get off your own f***ing asses and see for yourself! Well, he kept trying and was starting to piss me off, which he saw so he left. After his attempt to make me be all friendly with them again, as if nothing had happened, I had Alan came up to me gave me the same b******t as that tosser before. I was less abrupt with Alan as he was a mate, but he got the message and the message was simple: f**k them. I was out for a night with mates, and they didn't fit into that category. Even after all this Rich came up for one final attempt, to which he was basically told, 'F**k off and leave me alone.'

Well, here's a question to you readers: 'How would you have reacted in that situation?' Personally, I think that eighty-five per cent would have reacted like I did. Mind you, though, it's a good thing that these tossers are out of my life because they were ex-drinking partners and these dimwitted people wouldn't have understood that this new Del wasn't coming out on Leo Sayers (all-dayers) like he used to in the old days. In fact, this new Del wasn't even coming out more than once a month! So now they were out of my life I had eradicated another temptation to get back with Him. I don't know if this sounds like childish behaviour to you or not, but you must understand that this was a new, scary and difficult time for me; all dead wood had to be banished from my life for ever, and believe me these two w*****s were dead wood.

Well, I had a mixed reaction to my dumping of them tossers. Deb said, 'It's up to you, they're your mates (were).' Dez and Jas were a little more outspoken and said, 'Good on you, mate, and they can forget about speaking to us.' Dez was and still is angry and wants to bump into them so that he can give them a piece of his mind. Now you see, to me that is what you call good mates, whilst on the other hand we had Alan and Tina – well, mainly Tina – who thought I should text Craig and get together to sort it out. Sorry, Tina, but sort *what* out? As far as I'm concerned it's sorted. She even came up with some other b******t about had I thought that the reason they never visited me was that they wanted to remember me how I was before the stroke and not with all the tubes and stuff that was coming out of me. Yeah, good one, Tina, only one problem; I was in Salisbury Hospital for about three weeks with no tubes, no loss of memory and so on in fact I was all there, I could talk, see, hear; I wasn't a vegetable. Well, no matter what Tina said I wasn't budging and I must admit I was annoyed with her as I knew for a fact she'd reacted the same; she must have a pretty short memory because the time Alan was in hospital and it was only me and Dez who visited him she was hardly full of praise for the other people who she'd thought were Alan's mates. Yeah, I know people have their own opinions, but in my eyes Tina's was wrong and I felt let down, but then I'd get used to Alan and Tina's let-downs (more later).

Anyway, by now I was getting used to people's let-downs in general; maybe that's another reason why I stuck around with Him for so long because to me up until my stroke He'd never let me down. Him, yes; well how was I doing without Him around anymore? Pretty well, I thought; He wasn't in my thoughts constantly but He was occasionally and on one of these days I wrote down how I felt; may interest you, may not, but here's what I wrote:

> Bored, so bored I don't even want to do anything. This stroke has really f\*\*\*ed up my life. Every day seems like a struggle. I really do wish more and more that he had just finished the job he had started and killed me. I feel more and more depressed; I'm gradually slipping into deep depression. I give the impression that I'm happy but that's only on the outside; on the inside, my God, I'm so low. I'm so lonely I thought I had started to express my feelings but no, I'm still the same old Derek locked away in my own little world. I don't want to talk to anybody about how I feel, not even Deb. I'm fed up. I didn't ask to come into this world but I do have the choice to leave it. Silly talk, I know; but I have so many more thoughts about just going. I wish there was a place where you could see what the afterlife was like, I mean if I keep having thoughts of going more and more then why not just go? Am I going to be like this for ever? Or is it just a phase? I don't know, but if I knew it was for ever then just take me now, I beg of you; this is going to

be the hardest time of my life.

Well what do you think? Pretty strong stuff, and my feelings here were down to Him. He was trying to take over my mind again, but I was still fighting against Him. Big question is, though, 'Do I still feel like this at times?' The answer to that is simple. You see, the great gift that He has is that He turns boredom into excitement; oh yeah when you're with Him time just flies past and is never dull, but now the boredom has to be conquered by me and me alone, and at the moment is and believe me I will make every endeavour to make sure it continues like that!

# CHAPTER
## Fourteen

BACK TO MY rehabilitation; put simply it was going *great*. My brain and my legs were starting to get along really well, my arm was a little more uncooperative, but I knew in time with a bit of nagging from Deb and the OTs that my arm would also rekindle that old friendship with the brain.

But back to my walking, which as I said was picking up really well; so well, in fact, that Sam decided it was time for me to have a walking stick. Now this next bit may sound a bit sad and pathetic, but anyway I'm writing it. Well, a walking stick was great news; it meant I was one step closer to walking independently again, but with this great news there came a touch of sadness; yeah, the days of old Chipper had ended. He had served his time and done his duty; he had been a loyal and obedient servant and will be missed but never forgotten. I have quite childishly again named the walking stick (Willie) but it doesn't have the same effect as Chipper. See, told you it was pathetic – or is it? Because to me, any little thing no matter how pathetic is keeping my mind off Him, and anyway, you need a bit of tear-jerking emotion in a book, don't you?

Well, with things going smoothly there was soon coming up one of the most stressful situations us humans encounter during our lives; yeah, we'd soon be moving house. Now I've moved quite a few times in my life, but in the past I've had

*Return Ticket Please*

His help to aid me through the stress of a move. Oh yeah, whenever I've moved He's been there giving me His full support, and to be fair has never let me down, unlike what was to happen a couple of days before our move.

Now of course with the move Deb was feeling the most stress, but just sitting down and being on the sidelines can also be stressful, especially when you phone up the person who is going to be driving your removal van and they inform you that they can't drive the van any more, and to make matters worse they've known this for a while; great, f***ing marvellous. I mean, was it beyond you to let us know this as soon as you knew you wouldn't be able to drive the van? It wasn't just the fact that we'd lost the van driver, because along with the driver came the van. Are these people thick or what? This van and the driver had been promised to us for weeks and now, *boom!* Nothing except for me and Deb being left in the s**t. Hate it when people do that, they give it all the Charlie Potatoes saying, 'Yeah, yeah its not a problem everything's sorted,' and then let you down as if it's joke, well it f***ing ain't a joke, it's serious. But do you really know what made this let-down even worse? It was surprise; surprise caused by one of these so-called mates, you know the ones who before the stroke would do anything for you but now treat you like you're some f***ing leper. Well I f***ing ain't, and neither is Deb and the so-called mate was Paul – you know, the one whose wedding we went to. The excuse for his sudden change of mind was that he and his wife would be out of Salisbury for a couple of nights. *Lying f***ing bastard*; he was seen in the pub jollying it up with Alan and Tina (wanker).

Anyway, now this had happened me and Deb needed to

work fast; we needed a van and a driver in double quick time. Luckily enough for us, there was a woman who Deb knew and this woman's son had a van, an open-top van, but a van all the same. I mean, with time running out we weren't expecting a Pickford's removal van with gold doors on it, do you know what I mean? Anyway, for £50 we could have the van for a day. Now this was a problem as we didn't have £50 spare hanging around, so in our predicament there was only one thing to do and that was to ask Dot if she could lend us the cash. Dot being Dot there was only one answer she could give and that was yes, and she did. After all, parents don't like seeing their offspring struggling, do they? No matter how old and stupid (offspring that is) they are. (Thanks Dot.)

So now we've got the van sorted out our problems are still there because obviously a van with no driver is like having a TV with no electricity: useless. Well, we thought we could ask Alan. I wonder, because even Alan and Tina were now going down that road of has-been friends. Surprise, surprise, Alan's answer was no. I think he said he was working, which was fair enough – well, fair enough if he actually was, because I was starting to believe that all you could believe from Alan and Tina was nothing they said was the truth, and my suspicions were right as remember our move was the same day Jason saw Paul jollying it up with Alan and Tina in the pub.

So with these wasters out of the picture Deb and me had one hell of a problem. Jason asked his brother but he couldn't. I was even contemplating asking my brother, who hadn't driven for years. Believe me, my brother would have been a right long shot. With time running out and stuff being packed ready to be moved, Dez came up with a suggestion of someone: Vince, why don't you see if Vince can do it? Brilliant, Dez, why didn't I think of that? I'll give Vince a try. Good old Vincenzo. You remember Vince, the ex-drug addict I spoke about earlier? I'll tell you what, Vince was our last hope because nobody could think of anybody else. I don't mean that in a nasty way towards Vince, it's just that his name never came to mind until now.

Well, with Deb and Dez sitting there in the room anxiously waiting, I dialled Vince's number and prayed in my mind, 'Come on, Vince, please, please help your mate out.' I'm going to tell you now what a true bloody mate is. Vinny answered his phone and within ten minutes we had a driver, and thirty seconds of that ten minutes was Vince saying, 'Yeah, no problem mate,' and the rest of the time was spent giving him directions to where we lived and making sure over and over again that he was definitely not going to let us down, which he didn't and me thanking him over and over again. You see, *that's* a true mate being there when needed, most unlike these other twats Jas and Andy – Vinny excluded – who pop up into your life when they want something from you.

Well, there we go, we're sorted, we've got all we need. Yeah, it was one hell of a stressful time, mainly for Deb, but also me, and believe me, if this had happened in the old days I would have guzzled Him down by the litre and thought nothing about the stress because there wouldn't have been any; He would've made sure of that.

Anyway, our big day was here and it was going to be a bloody hard day's work, mainly for me. I'd be sitting there organising, making sure everyone was pulling their weight – nah, just joking. It was going to be a bloody hard day for Deb, Dez, David, Ben, Mandy, Vince and Sarah, who were basically stripping our house bare to fill up our new empty ground-floor flat. Well, it went really good and my thanks go to all those who helped. I just wish I could have been of much more assistance, but never mind there we go.

Now that we'd got the major problem of the move out of the way we had the decorating to do. This was no problem for Deb, as she absolutely loves decorating and she has got the place looking superb, although she has changed it round about twenty times and keeps going for, in her mind, what is perfection, but then again she is a Virgo, and this is what they are like. To me the place looks excellent.

Well, now that we've moved in and a vast majority of the decorating has been done, we – mainly Deb – also had our wedding to organise. I'll tell you what, talk about cramming everything into a short space of time! Well, me and Deb had already been to the registry office and booked a date. Yep, Miss Debbie Freeman would become Mrs Debbie Williams on 13 September. The organisation went as well as could be expected. We had Mandy and Sarah doing the food; Deb was being driven to the registry office by Graham (Mandy's husband); I was being driven there by Colin (Sarah's boyfriend). I was staying at Dezzie's the night beforehand – yeah, the organising did go as well as it could. We only had one minor problem and that was to get a hall and a disco for the reception, but that was luckily taken care of by Deb's ex-husband, Martin, and it was free.

Organising done there were, of course, the traditional

stag and hen nights to get out of the way. I certainly wanted a quiet stag night and I had one reason for wanting a quiet one: obviously because of Him. I mean, in the old days there would have been no question at all about me having a rowdy, booze-filled night on the piss with my mates and Him but not now. It would be too risky for me. I did have a couple of pints, but that was my limit. My mates had been warned that two pints were my limit, but to be honest I didn't feel like any more than two pints. In fact, one of my pints was a shandy. Now that would have been unheard of in the olden days:

*'Derek Williams has a two-pint limit and one pint is a shandy!'*
*'B******s I don't believe you!'*

I'll tell you what, He must have been really pissed off. I mean, here He's got another golden opportunity to lure me back into His seedy world and I've shunned Him; what do you think, another round to me? I think so. I enjoyed my sober stag night despite the so-called mates (Alan, Paul) not turning up, but at least I had my true mates there; there was me, my brother, Dez, Jas, Colin and Andy, and like I said, it was a good night. Oh, incidentally, Tina never turned up for Deb's hen night – surprise, surprise – but the non-appearance of Alan and Tina was nothing to what Tina had promised me and Deb for our wedding day. Oh yeah, at Paul and Rosie's wedding Tina had definitely had one of those moments where you open your mouth before you think. You see, at Paul and Rosie's reception Tina had promised me and Deb a whole salmon for the wedding reception's buffet, and yeah, get this: her and Alan were going to pay for me and Deb to stay the night in the White Hart Hotel on our wedding night. Ha! Good one, Tina! For Christ's sake, she couldn't even be bothered to turn up to the wedding! Yeah, one of our so-called best friends didn't come to our wedding. She claimed an illness prevented her from getting out of bed. B\*\*\*\*\*\*s, Tina. When your mouth opens it speaks so many lies; be careful of that, Tina, I think from now on if Tina is mentioned again I shall call her Cry Wolf. I'll give Alan his credit: he turned up at the reception for about half an hour, but I found it hard to talk to him because of all the false promises. Well, these two not turning up wasn't the only upsetting thing at our wedding: there was also Dot, which I'll come to later, but first of all I'll just tell you about the differences there were on the morning of this wedding and my previous one.

The first difference was waking up in Dez's house sober and not still under His influence from the night before's session. Then there was the difference of feeling a bit nervous, not mad with panic but just a few butterflies in my stomach. Then, of course, there was the fact that it would be me and only me who had to contend with these nerves; there would be no help from Him this time, as had been the case at my first marriage when, I'd drunk a bottle of wine an hour before the marriage; you know just a little bit of help from Him to get me through the actual marriage and carry me through to the reception (at Dot's) where He'd be in ample supply. Then there was the final difference, which was that this marriage was for *me*. He hadn't had a chance to f\*\*k with my mind and dictate what I was going to do in my life. Now this was so important to me, as my first marriage and my other girlfriends had all been based around Him, or to put it better, the major thing I'd have to decide on about going out with a girl would be what was the risk of them finding out about Him; if there wasn't a risk then they had a much better chance of going out with me. Yeah, I know that sounds very arrogant, but it's the best way I can think to put it. Nah, here's a better way: with Deb it was *me* who wanted to be her husband, it was *me* who loved her, it wasn't Him as had been the case before. What do you think, does that way sound better?

Anyway, we arrived at the registry office with my nerves building a bit more but still not going off the Richter Scale, and went through all the preliminaries, a lot of which I couldn't remember from my first marriage as He'd wiped them from my memory. Deb and me were in the little office with the registrar who actually did comment on how relaxed we both looked and then it was time, it was time for me and Deb to go out and face our friends and families and declare our love for each other. Well, I'm not going to bore you with the whole ceremony, I'll just tell you briefly how it went. Basically, I f***ed up the first line and me and Deb spent the rest of the ceremony giggling through it, like a couple of love-struck teenagers. But hey, we got through it we were now Mr and Mrs Williams. Now with me and Deb married it was time for the real fun to begin. Oh yeah, now senior Mrs Williams was going to step in and make sure everybody knew she was there.

Well, Dot had annoyed me and Deb very early in the proceedings by not even coming in and sitting down in the registry office; she claimed to me that she had felt claustrophobic and couldn't face sitting in that clammy room so she decided on witnessing our marriage from outside the room. Personally, I didn't believe the claustrophobic excuse; no, I put her childishness down more to the fact that her, Frank and brother had arrived late and everyone else was sitting in the registry office waiting for the marriage, while they were outside wondering where everyone else was. So you see, Dot being Dot would have taken it upon herself to stage a kind of one-woman protest, and all because she thought the whole world should wait for her; well I'm sorry, Dot; *you* were late, nobody else. To think that ten minutes before our marriage I'd started to get worried and asked Dez to go outside to see if you were there! Well, whatever her reasons were for not actually being in the room, Frank and my brother managed to confront and overcome the whole clamminess of the room. What do you think; am I being a bit pathetic? I don't think so, because she is family and for a mere twenty minutes at most you'd think she could have made the effort. I mean, was even my own flesh and blood turning into one of those so-called friends I'd had before the stroke?

Well, marriage over, Deb and me got all the congratulations and so on from everyone, but only from my brother in my family. Why? Well, Dot and Frank will say they ain't the sort of people to go in for all that kind of stuff; that's OK, fair enough, but I'm just asking for a shake of mine and Deb's hand and a simple word: 'congratulations'. I'm not asking for all the hugs, kisses and general over-the-top behaviour that you see from some families; no, just one simple word. Anyway, with the registry bit over it was onto the reception where once again Dot would announce she was there (even though she was leaving) but also make mine and Deb's wedding night a bit more special.

Well, the reception; yeah, it turned out to be quite eventful and for all the wrong reasons, which I'll come to later, but first of all I'll tell you about the drink limit I'd set for myself. As it was my wedding day, I thought I'd increase my intake of Him, but only by a celebratory glass of wine during the speeches. Yep that was the only addition to my standard two pints. On receiving my first pint more or less straight away, Dot said, 'I take it that's your only one?' I replied, 'No, Dot, it's not. It's my wedding day I'm going to have another pint later on.' She replied, 'WELL JUST MAKE SURE IT IS!'

I've put this in capital letters so as to signify the tone of voice it was said in. Well, as you know, in general if anybody is told that they'd better not do something they are going to do it, aren't they? I was no different, and as it was I had another pint and a half. Now if nothing had been said I would have stuck to the limit I'd set for myself. Now I know Dot was just showing her concern, but you must never say to an alcoholic, 'That's all you're having.' God, no! I'll tell you what, it was very lucky that I didn't go on a minesweeper expedition because that's what I felt like doing and He knew it; He knew my guard was down, could He take advantage of it? No, no he f***ing couldn't, because this little game of His has new rules and I'm making them now. What do you think, is that yet another round for me? Yeah, course it is.

Now I've picked on Dot a bit, but I do love her and she ain't bad at all as she showed at the reception when she said to me that her and my brother were going around to the

Red Lion Hotel to book me and Deb in for the night so as we had a treat on our wedding night. You know, the same treat as Alan and Cry Wolf had promised us (yeah right!). Now this was a lovely gesture from Dot and was really appreciated by me and Deb, but not trying to sound ungrateful, if I had the choice of having the night in the Red Lion or Dot congratulating me and Deb on our marriage, I'd take the congratulations. Never mind, it didn't work that way, did it?

Well, as I said, the night in the hotel was fully appreciated, but what Dot was to do next was most certainly not; in fact what she was to do next was to leave me ashamed and embarrassed.

As they say, here's how the story goes.

There was this bloke at the reception – I think his name was Tim. Now I'd never met him before, but it turned out that he'd also had a stroke, so obviously us two having gone through the same experience we got talking, me, him and Dez. Now I don't know why, but he told me and Dez that he'd picked up a vibe that Dot didn't really like Deb. Don't ask me how he got this vibe, because I don't know, but in all truthfulness it was something that me and Deb had felt for a while. Anyway, this Tim geezer said to me and Dez that he'd have a word with Dot and say to her that I'd get through what had happened with a lot of help and support from her and Deb (big mistake). Straight away on him saying this, both me and Dez told him, 'No, no – don't go over there and say anything to her because you don't know what she's like!' We told him this several times but would he listen? No, because as soon as he'd left me and Dez he was over there talking to her. Jesus Christ, the fat f***ing northern twat! Well, to be honest I knew that Dot wouldn't be too impressed with this total stranger talking to her about this stuff, but I certainly didn't expect her to react as she did, because with me, Dez and Jas sat down talking she nudged me on the shoulder and said in a very angry tone of voice, 'Right, that's it we're off! Give me a phone in the week,' and she stormed out with Frank and brother in tow.

Well I was fuming; I was fuming with that dickhead and I was fuming with Dot. I mean, it was mine and Deb's wedding day; couldn't she just bite her tongue for once? With all this commotion guess who was calling out? Yeah, of course it was Him, and I must be totally honest: I obeyed Him, I had His comforting arms around me in the form of another pint – definitely a round to Him, but only just, because even though He had come to my assistance in this situation, I wasn't going to crumble, despite the enormous pressure He was putting me under to continue enjoying the so-called help He was giving me. No, I wasn't going to give up to Him this time, I'd been down that road before and look where it had got me.

Anyway, with all this happening and me succumbing to Him a bit you'd be forgiven for thinking that this was a shit day; it wasn't, because at the end of the day the only important thing was that me and Deb got married, which we did. So in all honesty, apart from if somebody had died at the wedding, nothing else was really that important, was it?

# CHAPTER
# Fifteen

HAVE I BORED you yet? Well, if I have I'm sorry, but I'm going to continue anyway. I'm going to move back onto my cognitive therapy. Yeah, I'm going to talk about something that is very important to anybody in everyday life. The next challenge on my agenda would be to go into town on my own, not straight away but after Jo had taken me in a couple of times to make sure I'd be safe on my own.

Now going into town on my own probably sounds very trivial to you, but believe me it's not. You see, what you have to understand is that I hadn't done this for weeks and on top of this we'd moved house – oh yeah, and I'd had a brain haemorrhage. You see, to me it wouldn't be a simple jump on the bus, wander round town, do what you got to do and then hop back on the bus home. No, to me it had to be explained, it had to be explained where to get the bus from where I lived, it had to be explained where to get off the bus from town, all these things had to be – well, how can I put it? – drummed into my head. On top of all these things, I had roads to contend with, I had people rushing around, all these things that we take for granted and are part of everyday life were now to me another obstacle. Having said all this, I did feel pretty confident about going into town with Jo or Deb because you see my confidence for me going into town on my own had been damaged a little bit. You see,

I'd set little targets for me to achieve in my build-up to letting me loose to go into town on my own. One of these little targets was to go up to our local shop on my own after having gone up with Deb a few days beforehand to show me the way of course. What do you think, all sounds pretty easy, doesn't it? I mean, the shop's only at most a ten-minute walk away; of course it's easy, I mean even a blind, brainless buffoon could do that, couldn't they?

Not if they went the wrong way they couldn't, as I did. I started walking in the complete wrong direction. What made it even worse is that there were only two directions to go: one to the shop, two to I don't know where. Well, as it happens I was very lucky as Deb had caught sight of me from the window and came to my rescue. We had a good giggle about it but in all seriousness if I couldn't find our local shop on my first expedition out on my own, how the hell was I going to go from our house to town and back again?

So as you can well understand, this is why I constantly had to be told which bus to get, where to get off and so on, and so on. Basically, I had to be told what, when and where. As I said, part of the rehab was for Jo to take me into town and set me little tasks like buying a stamp, crossing busy roads and climbing up and down stairs – oh and of course trying to get me to use an escalator. Now I've conquered a lot of challenges since my stroke but I'm afraid to say the escalator defeated me; I never really liked them before the stroke and I hate them even more now. If I'm perfectly honest, I don't care whether I do another escalator or not.

Well, with these little trips with Jo proving a success she told me and Deb that she had full confidence in me going to town on my own; trouble was, though, I'd already been into town on my own. Yeah, I'd gone into town on my own when Deb was out for the day in Winchester doing some Christmas shopping. Risky? Nah, I didn't think so because I was very confident that I could do it; notice I've said that I felt confident that I could do it, well that is because Deb didn't know I was going into town on my own. I didn't tell Deb I was going to face the town trip alone because she was out for the day and I didn't want her to spend her day out worrying about me, so I thought best to keep quiet and anyway it was Christmas; there were presents to buy, weren't there? And then, of course, there was Him; I mean, if I was just sat at home twiddling my thumbs and picking my nose He would undoubtedly enter into my mind, so what better way to combat that than my doing my own little thing? My trip into town went really good; there were no mishaps, no dramas and I bought Deb a really nice bottle of perfume. I did tell Deb when she'd got back from Winchester what I'd done and she said, 'Yeah, I thought you would do that!' Well anyway, it'd been done; I had now proved I could go into town alone, which was great, but Deb wasn't just worried about me getting lost or injured in town; no, Deb also had worries about me going back to Him in the form of the pub or off-license. As I've said before, I'd hate to be the person who's back at home waiting for their recovering alcoholic partner to get back home without any signs that they've been drinking! Of course, the more and more I go into town Deb's worries have subsided, but will they disappear for ever?

Anyway, with me now being safe to go into town on my

own I can really be considered virtually independent. Yeah, I have the walking stick, my left arm is ignored sometimes and I may get confused quite easily; but all in all I consider myself independent.

Now with all these things happening and progress really being made I noticed another change in me; I noticed now that I would speak my mind more than what I'd have done with Him. I was now starting to let my voice be heard about things that p****d me off or annoyed me. I wasn't going into a mad rage, I was just letting my opinion be heard. Why this change in me? Simple: I didn't have to protect Him anymore, I didn't have to have that self-discipline that I'd had to keep for years so as to keep my secret affair with Him under wraps. I tell you what, it doesn't half feel good letting off a bit of steam knowing that it's *you* letting off that steam and not Him, or just keeping quiet in the fear that somebody may get a bit suspicious as to why I'd be losing it every day.

I think the main targets of my steam-releasing have been bus drivers; man do they piss me off or what! I think elderly people or other walking stick users will understand where I'm coming from here. The problem with bus drivers is simple: why don't they wait? By this I mean, why don't they wait for us to sit down before they continue their journey; what's a twenty-second wait compared to a few hours' wait, which is what it would be if someone got injured due to their impatience? I was very nervous the first few times I got on to a bus on my own, and even though my leg is getting stronger I am still a little bit apprehensive about them and will not get on a bus if it looks too full to me. Now this probably sounds all very silly and unimportant to a lot of you, but I'm just trying to give you an insight into little things that us with disabilities have to contend with, and being a stroke victim it's another obstacle our recovering brain has to cope with; and believe me, it's not easy, it's scary.

Well, I think you may have gathered from a bit of the last passage I wrote that it was Christmas time. Yes, it was the season to be jolly, the season where the majority of us go well overboard on His hospitality, but for me this Christmas time was going to be very different because of course I was going to be in the minority; I was going to be in that group of people who are on the outside. I was going to be in the group of people who stay sober at Christmas time.

*What? What? Derek Williams staying sober at Christmas time? Never, I don't believe it, he'll never do it, there'll be too much temptation around for him!*

Now of course there was a lot of temptation around me, but I'd seen people stay sober at Christmas time. I'd seen my brother stay sober many Christmas times, I'd seen um, um... let me think a moment... OK then, that's it; my brother is the only person I can remember who I'd seen sober at Christmas time but that didn't mean I couldn't stay sober, did it? If my brother could then I could, and anyway, with me it wasn't a question of would I, wouldn't I; it was simpler than that, wasn't it? I *had* to. I couldn't take that risk of getting pissed just once and leaving a slight opening in my defences for Him to exploit, could I?

Obviously at this time of the year Deb's concerns about Him being so close to me were heightened; I mean, just because I couldn't indulge myself in the games that me and Him used to play it didn't mean that it had to be spoiled for everyone else, did it? By this I mean should there have been alcohol in the house? Well, I suppose there will be different views on this, but my own view personally is yes, of course there should have. Why should other people's enjoyment be spoiled by my problem? So, as it was He was in the house over the Christmas period – not in the vast amounts that I'd witnessed as a child or as an adult, but in a very minute proportion. I think the amount of alcohol that we'd bought in would have lasted me about two days in my hay day. Christ I'd never seen a place so bare of alcohol during the Christmas period! But hey, it was for a good reason, wasn't it?

Anyway, the big question was how would I cope with even the minimum of temptation if, for example, I were left in the house on my own with His voice beckoning me over? This situation did occur once, and even though His voice did try and penetrate my defences I stood firm and ignored Him. I had to, I wanted to, I needed to; I'd let Him back into my life too many times and I was determined that this wasn't going to happen again. I knew that if I could get through Christmas time sober I would have achieved so much. In a weird sense, if I stayed sober at Christmas time to me it would've meant more than learning to walk again, that is how much He'd poisoned me.

*I did, I did it!* Despite the fact that I'd been so close to those demons who I'd spent so many child and adult Christmases with, I conquered them again. This was another round to me and a big one. Did He or has He enough gas left in the tank to win this fight?

As I've said on numerous occasions, my rehab was going brilliantly. I'd learnt the basics of walking again; I'd noticed I had a left arm; I'd been into town on my own and I'd even managed to do some form of dancing on that night out at the Chicago Rock. With all these achievements under my belt you may be thinking, 'Well what else is there to do?' Well, another part of my rehab was going to once again mainly involve my brain and my left arm. This part of my rehab was going to involve something that I was not a stranger to; it was going to involve something I'd spent the majority of my working life doing. It was of course to cook a meal for Deb, under the supervision and watchful eye of another one of my OTs (Lynne). Lynne would come round to our place and I'd show my culinary prowess.

I think the first time she came round my menu of poached egg on toast was a little bit of a let-down because I think the whole idea of this exercise was to get me planning out and preparing a meal a little bit more advanced than a six-year-old could do. Nevertheless, even though my choice of meal – or should I say snack – was basic, Lynne made sure that my left arm was in full use. Oh yeah, as soon as I started favouring my stronger, natural right arm I'd soon be reminded that my left arm wasn't just there for show. Anyway, with my very basic snack of poached egg on toast a success, I still thought I'd achieved something. After all, I didn't burn or cut myself, which in a kitchen is an achievement itself, and let's face it, there are definitely people out there – blokes mainly – who wouldn't have a clue where to start on the good old poached egg on toast.

Well, with Lynne's slight disappointment at my first meal I decided I'd do something a little more adventurous the next time she was be coming. For my next choice of culinary wizardry I chose to do stuffed tomato. Now this would involve more brainwork, more use of my left arm and in general more awareness than my simple poached egg. Let me run you through the ingredients and the preparation. God, I'm making this sound like a Gordon Ramsey three-course extravaganza, not a paltry stuffed tomato; well, to me it did feel like a three-course extravaganza. Well, here goes:

*Ingredients*

*Beef steak tomato*
*Garlic clove*
*Spring onion*
*Sliced ham*
*Long-grain rice*
*Mature cheddar cheese*

Well there we go: there's our simple list of ingredients, now let's get on with the preparation, which of course may sound pretty simple to your average everyday person, but as we all know I wasn't one of them.

*Preparation*

*Cut tomato in half and using a teaspoon scoop out seeds and centre of the tomato. (Now this was particularly tricky for me as it meant I had no choice but to use my suspect left arm. It went really well and I'll say this, for all my ignoring my left arm my left hand has quite good control.)*

*Stick on saucepan of water and bring to the boil. When boiling add rice and cook (I don't use measurements).*

*While the rice is cooking finely chop up your garlic, ham and spring onion.*

*When your rice is cooked mix it in with your finely chopped garlic, ham and spring onion and season.*

*Put your scooped out tomato into the oven and leave for about five to ten minutes just to soften up a bit.*

*When this is done put your rice mixture into your tomato, making sure you squeeze in quite tightly.*

*Top your tomato with your grated cheese and stick in oven until cheese is melted and browned.*

*Serve.*

Well, there we have it: not exactly a grade one, cost-you-£20 meal in a top-notch restaurant, but nevertheless its a nice little meal/snack that hopefully with the way that I've explained it anyone could do. Now you may be thinking, 'Well what's the importance of all this "can he cook" a meal malarkey?' This is a very important part of your rehab, as probably the most dangerous room in your house is your kitchen. The reason for the OT coming up wasn't to see if this old qualified chef had lost any of his cooking prowess or magic, she wasn't coming up to taste the fruits of my toil in the kitchen; no, she was coming up to observe how safe I was in a kitchen should I choose to cook a meal for Deb on my own (which I have) without any help or another pair of eyes making sure that I wasn't about to chop my finger off or knock a boiling saucepan off the oven top. Well, my OT was happy that it would be safe to let me loose in a kitchen on my own, so there we had it. I'd passed another one of my little tests that were leading me towards the goal of total independence.

Obviously there were a few differences between me in a kitchen now and the older days where at Don Giovanni's I'd have about ten checks on the board and ten saucepans on the stove with my brain thinking ten to the dozen and my hands working just as fast. I was obviously slower, I was ultra careful, I was cooking at my pace; but do you know what the *major* difference was? The major difference was He wasn't around to guide me through. You see, probably about ninety-nine per cent of my catering life, whether it be at work or at home, He'd been involved. Whenever I'd had a saucepan on the go, stirring a sauce or even just chopping up parsley He would be by my side in whichever disguise He chose. This might be in the form of a pint of lager, a bottle of wine or brandy to take that sneaky gulp from or in the form of a more leisurely, social can of whatever. How the f\*\*k I managed to cook for about fifty to a hundred people on a regular basis at Don Giovanni's is beyond me.

There's an interesting question I have asked myself on occasions. 'Would I have been able to cook for that same amount of people without Him?' I guess the answer to that question is no, because on the numerous occasions I've cooked for girlfriends at home He's been at my side. I mean, cooking for one person (girlfriend) is a non-pressurised situation in the catering world, but oh no He'd be there whether it was in the disguise of an out-in-the-open social view or in the form of a quick-nip-up-to-the-bedroom-gulp-Him-down sort of way. Even the workplaces where there was no chance of drinking I'd have enough of Him in my bloodstream to last the day.

So this cooking on my own was definitely a new experience, and I'd be lying if I said I'd never thought about asking Him to join me for another meal, but there's a great difference between thinking and doing, so I'm just happy to leave it at that and prove to myself and Him that my will is stronger than before.

In this chapter I've mentioned work; now this is something that would have to be thought about, not immediately, but all the same the wheels would soon be in motion.

# CHAPTER
## Sixteen

NOW WITH ALL that's happened over the last year you'd think I'd be itching to get back to work and achieve full independence; well, I'm sorry to say I'm not. Do you know why I'm scared? I'm scared because of Him. He was a major part of my working life – well, probably the most major part of it. I'm also scared because I don't know what to do for a living. I've been given a second chance and I'm stumped as what to do. It's like I'm sixteen again; you know, that age where we decide the career we wish to earn our living from. What the hell am I going to do? I mean, most of my working life has been involved in catering and there's absolutely no chance I could or would go back to that again because I don't think I would be able to cope in a kitchen physically and also I don't think I'd be able to cope mentally. I think the physical side is self-explanatory and obviously I'm seen able by people, but the mental side is a little more difficult for people to comprehend. I think the major problem mentally of course lies with Him. Because I'd be on my own with no Him to guide me, my confidence would be at an all-time low and my insecurities at an all-time high. Now I'm not joking here, but with these two combined I'd need help, and as we know in the past the help would come from His wise old head. But now where would it come from? Exactly; at the moment I don't know either. So at the present time I'm a bit vulnerable, He is playing on my mind as time for that big lunge back into working life draws closer. One thing I know for sure is that whatever job I decide upon it has to be as least stressful as it possibly can be. There cannot be the slightest chink in my armour for Him to exploit.

Another thing I'll have to adjust to is getting used to the set routine that working life brings along with it. I mean, how will I cope with the routine of getting up, going to work, working, coming home from work? In the old days He would deal with the boredom of this same day-in, day-out routine. Don't get me wrong; I do and have had a routine since my return home from hospital, but it's *my* routine and is done how I wish it to be done; there is absolutely no pressure on me whatsoever.

Another worry is how will the new people I meet take to me or vice versa? Let's remember, it's just me they'll be meeting now, not me and Him. How will they react to my life over the past year and a half? I talked to my OT, Jo, about whether I should mention being an alcoholic, and even though she said it was up to me, she was hinting not to mention it, which at first I thought would be for the best but the more I think about it then the more I have decided that I will tell people about my alcoholism. I hid Him for so many years; now my secret's out of the bag I'm not going to cover up for Him anymore. To not say anything about Him and keep Him hidden is to be ashamed; I didn't tell people before because a massive part of me was ashamed and scared of people's reaction. I'm not scared or worried about people's reactions now because at the end of the day, the people who are most important in my life know about my alcoholism and they are the ones who count! So now when I'm asked why I had a brain haemorrhage at such a young age I shall tell them about being an alcoholic and let them deal with it in whatever way they wish to!

# CHAPTER
# Seventeen

WELL, AS I'VE said, the wheels to getting me back to work were in motion; the moment I'd been dreading for months and months was no longer a dot in the distance, it was here staring right in front of me. My holiday (yeah, right!) was over. I've jokingly said to people, 'I know I wanted a nice long break from work, but this is ridiculous!' When I told Dot and Frank that Jo was mentioning work, Frank jokingly said, 'Oh, that'll be a relapse then!' (Cheek!)

So what are the steps that are being taken to get me back to work? Well, obviously it's not like any normal person who is out of work. I mean, I can't just nip down the Job Centre or phone up a job advertised in the situations vacant section, so as this is a totally new experience for me, the hospital – well, Jo – has been helping and advising me on the different options there are. One of the options to come up is to do a bit of voluntary work to ease me back into a working routine without stress. This sounds good to me because as a volunteer you don't have the pressure of a paid job; well, at least I don't think so, because as time nears He's poking His head into my thoughts again.

I'll try to clarify what He's done to me as best I can. If I won a £1,000,000 on the lottery my feelings would be, 'Yeah, great a £1,000,000 – so what?' The reason for my delayed response is that despite the fact that me, Deb and the kids would be sorted for life, it would be a life without Him. It would be and is hard to know that the family could celebrate with a few drinks but for me that would be a no-no. Now believe me that is the hardest thing for an alcoholic to come to terms with; the fact that in a situation where there is celebrating to be done they simply can't join in, and I do mean can't. They'll want to, because I know I certainly would want to, but I couldn't for the risk of Him getting His claws into me again. It's for these reasons and thoughts I still have about Him that I'm going to be assigned a key worker from ADAS (Alcohol and Drugs Advisory Service). Now this is something I'd never dreamt of doing in the past, but on talking to Jo and Deb it seems the sensible thing to do, although I don't think this situation would ever have occurred if my secret hadn't been revealed to Jo, because once again she had assumed that my haemorrhage was caused by binge drinking. Do you know that brain haemorrhages are becoming more and more common in younger people, especially women, due to binge drinking?

Anyway, when I'd been to see Jo for a session I asked her if she knew what caused the haemorrhage and this is when she told me about the binge drinking facts. Think I was a bit naive or stupid – or was I still trying to protect Him or too ashamed to admit to my past with Him? – because it wasn't until I'd finished my session and told Deb what had happened when Deb said, 'She (Jo) doesn't know the whole truth about you; Dr Walters doesn't know the whole truth. You'll have to tell Jo and see what she says, because you could turn back to Him just like that.' What Deb said here was very true, because how would or will I cope if a problem occurs which I don't think I could handle without His help? Yeah, I know I have Deb to help me, but He doesn't work like that because He'll make me bottle it up and then let me reveal my problem when He's ready; well, at least that's what used to happen, but will it ever again?

Well, as it happened I had another session with Jo the following week in which she wanted Deb to attend as well, because this session was once again talking about work options.

Me and Deb had discussed it and it was agreed that now was the time to reveal all to Jo because there was no way that Deb would be happy about me going back to work with Jo only knowing half the truth. There was also another reason for Deb's worries; she also wanted to go back to work, because as Deb had put it, there's only so much cleaning that you can do, because let's not forget here, Deb has also been off work for over a year. Yeah, she'd looked after me and been everywhere with me when I came out of hospital, but now I was independent enough to look after myself. How hard this must have been for Deb; she worried about me being alone all day, worried about me going up the shop; should she give me the right amount of money as to stamp out any temptation of me wandering around the alcohol section and maybe, just maybe, taking that first step towards my old days? Did she have enough trust in me that this wouldn't happen? If it did happen, would she know that I was once again dancing with the Devil?

Well, the time had come to spill the beans to Jo about my secretive past. Jo had barely started talking about work options when Deb said to her, 'Everyone has put Del's haemorrhage down to binge drinking, but the reason for it was that he's an alcoholic.' Well, there we go, it's out in the open now. I think Jo was a little shocked but we all talked. I explained to Jo that He was a massive part of my working life and I had real, major concerns about Him coming back into my life when I began work again. Deb explained her worries about her going back to work. Jo asked, 'Do you think you'll go back to Him again?' And I said, 'Well, I can sit here and say no way, there's no chance of that happening again, but I'd only be saying that to keep everyone happy; the truthful answer is I don't know.'

It was during these discussions that Jo mentioned ADAS and I reluctantly said I'd talk to them. I say reluctantly because I'm of the belief that just because there would be someone there for me to talk to, someone who I take it has also gone through the experience of alcoholism, it wouldn't mean *boom!* that's it, you're cured. I mean, as beneficial as it may be talking to someone with the same experiences, they are not me. Their reason for alcoholism is most probably different than mine; I mean, I've written down at the start of the book that I think the reason for my alcoholism was boredom, but is that really the reason, or is there something else that caused it? So to be blatant about it, do I really know why I became an alcoholic? Do these people from ADAS really know why they became alcoholics? Yeah, I know that people with addiction problems find it a massive help talking to people who have – how can I put it? – 'been there, done that, bought the T-shirt', but would I? You're probably sat there thinking, 'What a cynical view you have about these addiction helpers,' and you'd be right, but why do I have this view? Is it maybe that He's still there in my subconscious telling me that these people don't know what they're on about, telling me that it's Him I need, not them? Is it just my stubbornness; you know, me thinking that I need nobody's help; I can do this on my own? Well, if that's the case I'd be thick, because let's not forget I've had a go at trying to get Him out of my life on my own and it didn't get me very far, did it?

As I said, I agreed to Jo contacting them and getting the ball rolling, and boy was that ball rolling, because a couple of days after Jo contacted them I received a letter saying that there'd be someone up in a couple of weeks to begin proceedings. I must admit, when I received the letter I felt good, it gave me the feeling that I wasn't on my own. I was warming to the idea of talking to someone who would be able to understand my problem. I don't mean that badly in a way to anyone else who I've talked to about it – especially Deb – but as Deb's admitted, she doesn't understand what it's like to be an alcoholic.

Well now, knowing that I had someone coming up to talk to me about it I needed to ask them some questions about their own experiences; you know, in a way it would be like me being the counsellor for a bit. I mean, it wasn't going to be any good to me talking to someone who hasn't been there, was it? I'd been doing that since my alcoholism was revealed.

Well, my major question was going to be plain and simple: why do you think you become an alcoholic? This was to be a set-the-ball-rolling question which would then be followed by others, except I never got as far as asking my first question because literally about ten minutes before the man from ADAS was due to arrive they appeared, the flashing lights which are my warning sign that a fit will occur. Can you believe it, of all the times for this to happen it had to happen now! Well, that was it, wasn't it? I took diazepam to control it but the lights didn't go away so I took another two. I remember the bloke coming in and helping Deb get me settled, but that was it; the diazepam had taken their effect and I was in the land of nod.

As usual, I woke up in my confused state as I do after a fit and take about a minute to realise where I am or what's happened, then asked Deb what the bloke had said. Basically, what he had said was that I would be put on a list and assigned a key worker in due course. I am still waiting for my key worker, despite being on the high priority list; feel sorry for the people on the low priority list, if there is such a thing.

Without this help and support from a key worker my enthusiasm to rush out into working life hasn't really appeared. These concerns about work and alcohol have been talked over with Jo on numerous occasions, and yeah while it is nice to talk to someone who is not as close to me as Deb and my family, I do wonder if the problem is fully understood. I mean, I don't think *I* fully understand it! Why is it that in the past despite the warning signs I still hung around with Him? Well anyway, there is only so much talking you can do about Him; there has to be a cut-off point where you have to say to yourself, 'Right, come on, now the time is here to get back into the boring routine of work.' Some of you reading this may be thinking, 'Oh come on, you lazy bastard, get off your fat ass and get a job and stop hiding behind your alcoholism.' Well, to these people I simply say f\*\*k off and put my shoes on, be inside my f\*\*\*ing head for a day and you'll soon understand where I'm coming from.

As it was, Jo suggested to me that it might be an idea to think about voluntary work. Notice I say 'suggested', because now nobody was telling me what to do. It sounded like a good idea; I mean, there surely wouldn't be any pressure or stress involved in voluntary work, would there? Once again He was discussed, but Jo said to me to take my time and think about it. I said, 'OK, I'll tell you what, give me a month to get my head around this massive step in my life and I'll contact you and we'll get the ball rolling.'

Now believe me, this was going to be a massive step; this would be like announcing to the world that I was there; my journey had been completed I was now back to how things used to be; I was now a regular member of society. The phrases 'get things back to how they used to be' and 'get things back to normal' would pop up frequently, but these phrases were wrong, as I pointed out to Deb and Jo, because I didn't want things back to how they used to be or back to normal, because that meant being back with Him, didn't it? So things now had to be different, this was now going to be a new life.

Well, as that month dwindled away I would have mixed feelings. Sometimes I would think, *God, shit! What's going to happen? I really don't need this work crap – why do I need it? I'm happy just as I am, I'm not bored, I'm safe from Him – why rock the boat, why put everything I've done in jeopardy just for a few quid at the end of the week? What's the big thrill about going out to work and meeting new people? What's more important my safety or a wage packet?* Then we had the other side of the coin where I'd think, *Yeah, I'm looking forward to this, this is going to be great, it's a new start and I'm not going to f\*\*k up this time.* So I was having mixed feelings and was pretty confused, but no matter how my feelings were, I'd said to Jo that I'd contact her in a month so contact her I did.

Jo arranged to come to my place and discuss further the voluntary work outlay; once again His name came up and was discussed. I still had no word from ADAS, which was a bit annoying for me and Deb.

(Oh, just quickly I have now got an appointment through for 26 August, which is good news.)

Well anyway, back to Plan Work. I didn't have a clue where or what I wanted to volunteer as, so I was just waiting for Jo to throw some ideas around and when that little bell went off in my head I'd pipe up and say, 'Yeah, I like the sound of that I'll give that a go.' Of course it wasn't that easy; Jo would have to contact the place and then I'd have to go down with her to scout the place over and also for them to give me the once over. I suppose in a way it was like some kind of interview, but an interview where there'd be no pressure.

Well, Jo threw some ideas around, one of which was to volunteer working with animals; you know, like walking a dog for somebody who can't walk it themselves. For some reason that little bell went off in my head and I said, 'Yeah, I like the idea of that.' Not really sure why that appealed to me, because I've never had a dog in my life – in fact the only pet I've ever had is a gerbil. The only conclusion I can think of as to why I liked the idea so much is that you can talk to animals and they don't judge you; animals don't care whether you're an alcoholic, heroin addict or come to think of it they don't even care if you're a mass murderer. I suppose another reason is that animals don't ask you questions about your past or in my case about my drinking; don't get me wrong, I don't mind being asked questions about my alcoholism, but I do tend to sense that when some people, not all, ask questions about it, it is for the pure and simple reason that somewhere along the line of me answering the question they will try to shift the conversation onto a problem of theirs. Excuse me, you've asked me the question, at least have the decency to *listen* to my answer. I've listened to other people's problems all my life, now just for once listen to my problem.

A person named in this book, Tina – remember her? – aka Cry Wolf, is a past master at this. Her solution to my problem is to say, 'Don't ever go back to drinking or you'll lose me as a friend.' And then after her pathetic threat it's a half-hour talk on what a bad stomach she had the other night; what a fake person. I'm sorry, but don't ask me anything about my alcoholism if you don't want to hear the answer. It's funny really, but when these situations occur I'm like two people; there's the person you can see listening, trying to look interested, and then there's the person in my head saying, 'Yeah, yeah shut the f**k up, you're boring me to death, your bad stomach is not a problem.'

Anyway, back to work. Jo contacted a place for this voluntary work with animals, but there was a problem and quite a big one, because walking dogs wouldn't be practical for me considering the walking stick and my unsteadiness on my feet, so that was that one out of the window. So with that idea dismissed, Jo suggested I do something like work in a day care centre as I'm supposed to have, as Jo and Deb have put it, good communication skills. Personally I've never noticed it, but then I suppose the majority of us never realise the little things we are good at, but hey don't we realise the things we're bad at!

Well, Jo suggested a place that might be the thing that I was just looking for. The name of the place was The Jo Benson Day Centre. Jo asked how I felt about it and was I ready for this massive change to my life. I know there might be a few of you out there thinking, 'Get it together, you skiver, and get off your ass and get back to work after all you're better now.' Well *no*, no I'm not better yet, my physical side is probably at about seventy-five per cent of what it used to be and my mental side is – well, well I wouldn't like to put a percentage on that, but its safe to say that's it's way below seventy-five per cent.

Despite all my worries, I did think that people would be thinking that I was just skiving, and even though everything was now up to me and I could take as much time as I wanted, this thought of people thinking I was just skiving prompted me into asking Jo to contact the day centre. Now this was a really big step, but it had to be taken at some point and despite my thoughts of, *Shit this is it, mate, this is your first real step back into working life and it's going to be a working life without Him.* I realised I'd reached that point. It was still going to be a little bit of time before I'd get an appointment and visit the centre for my sort of interview, but it was time that was getting shorter and shorter. I'd spend the time thinking to myself that I'd have to be strong; no matter what happened, good or bad, He was not allowed to get to me, which sounds easy in theory but in reality was and will be a lot harder because He's a sneaky bastard, He gives you no warning, He can take over your life just like that!

Well, a couple of weeks had passed and then I got it, I got a phone call from Jo to arrange an appointment to say she'd come up to my house and fill me in on what had been occurring and where we were going from there and basically to double-check that I was still up for it, which I suppose I was. Please try to understand my lack of enthusiasm, but the thought of going back to work without His company was scaring me shitless. Jo filled me in on what she knew about the day centre and what sort of things the voluntary work would involve, and I must admit, the way that Jo put it made it sound quite good. She made it sound – how can I put it? – relaxing, yeah relaxing and non-pressurised.

Deb, who has been a rock through all of this, also agreed that the day centre would be a good starting block for me, so with everything that had been discussed I one hundred percent and wholeheartedly asked Jo to make an appointment with the day centre. Jo said that when an appointment had been made she would accompany me to the centre so as to fill them in on the situation and as a bit of moral support.

Well, about another week passed and Jo had arranged an appointment for me at the day centre; I can't remember the date or time of the appointment, but the appointment had been made. Jo arranged to pick me up and now was to begin

*Return Ticket Please*

the next chapter in an eventful sixteen months.

On the day of my interview I was nervous, I was very nervous; obviously this wasn't the first time I've been nervous in my adult life, but it was the first time I'd been nervous knowing that He wouldn't be by my side. This was a totally new experience and not a nice one. I was all alone now and I couldn't, as I used to, just nip off to get Him and glug Him down so as to make my nerves disappear; oh no, these nerves were here to stay and I'd have to deal with them on my own, and of course I knew that this wouldn't be the only time in the rest of my life where I'd have to conquer these feelings.

It was good that Jo came because that made me feel a bit calmer, and it also meant that she could explain the whole situation rather than me mumbling and stuttering over what had happened over the past sixteen months.

On arriving, Jo asked how did I feel, was I nervous? I said I was fine, which I may have looked on the outside, but boy on the inside the old butterflies were flapping their wings frantically, a feeling I'd been devoid of for the last few years thanks to Him.

Anyway, the interview type thing was to be with a lady called Janice; we went into her office and Jo explained the situation, she told Janice what had happened and how well I'd done in physio and OT and that we felt it was time for me to move onto the next stage of my rehab, which was to do this voluntary work as a stepping stone towards proper employment. Janice explained what sort of things the volunteers do; these were things such as serving tea and coffee, serving lunch and clearing up and probably the most important thing of all, talking to people. I told Janice about my epilepsy, which she was cool about, but the one thing which wasn't mentioned was my alcoholism, and it still hasn't been, not yet. The reason this hasn't been mentioned is because I haven't been asked if the doctors knew why I had the haemorrhage; if I'm asked then I will tell them about my alcoholism, but until then I will keep silent. You may think, 'Yeah, but keeping silent means He still has a stranglehold over you, and you did say earlier that you wouldn't keep your alcoholism a secret so as to be released from that stranglehold.' To that I say you could be right, but what will your opinion be if I say, 'I'm not ashamed of being an alcoholic but I'm not proud of it either. I can't change what has happened, so what benefit would I be getting by just announcing my alcoholism within five minutes of meeting someone? As I've said, I will tell people about it if I'm asked what caused the haemorrhage, but I'm not about to start shouting it from the rooftops either.

Well, back to my interview. After speaking to Janice for about twenty minutes we agreed that I would come in and help out every other Monday; doesn't sound like much, does it? But to me it was like, 'Shit one day's work every two weeks is like full-time employment.' This wasn't being lazy, this was me trying to get my head around the reality of how far I'd come. This was me realising that the biggest challenge of my life was getting closer and closer to ending. This also made me think about what I would do if life got boring again. Would I set myself new challenges? Or would I take the chicken's way out and go back to Him? Another one of my worries was how would I reschedule my life so as to keep

*Return Ticket Please*

my routine going? Well, these would be things I'd have to deal with my way.

When we'd finished talking to Janice, she asked Sarah, another volunteer, to show us around so I could meet some of the people there. My God that was nerve-racking, I mean what was I to say, how would these new people take to me or me to them? Well, luckily enough a lady called Pauline came up to me and took me under her wing. She introduced me to a few of the people there, telling them I'd be coming as a volunteer in a couple of weeks. It made it easier but I still felt a bit of a plonker standing there just saying, 'Yeah I'll see you in a couple,' to whoever I was introduced.

One of the ladies I was introduced to was Joyce, and she is a lovely old dear who is eighty years old. Joyce was the only one I had a real conversation with. Poor little Joyce had a haemorrhage when she was just twenty-nine and as a result of her haemorrhage she has never been able to use her right hand. Now that must be hard. I've seen her hand and her fingers are just clenched shut. You can certainly see how much better off we are nowadays. If Joyce had had her haemorrhage later on in the century, with physio she'd have been able to use her right hand. My left hand was just like Joyce's after my haemorrhage, but with the hard work that's been put in at physio my left hand/arm is probably at about seventy-five per cent of what it was before the haemorrhage.

While I was talking to Joyce she showed me what she had been doing. Well, I'll tell you what, it was amazing what she'd been doing because she'd been doing one of them cross-stitch tapestry things and all just with her left hand. Now that is amazing. Can you imagine the patience she must have to do that? I understand a little bit of what Joyce is going through – I say little bit because I was lucky enough to have the use of both hands. I didn't use my left as much as I should have because my brain wouldn't allow it at first, but more and more it's getting there, but poor Joyce has been dependant on her left hand for fifty-one years. Just to get an idea of what it's like in Joyce's world, put one of your arms in a sling for a day and see how hard, if even possible, the simplest of tasks are. I bet you any money that all of you will take that sling off at some point of the day through frustration. Just think yourselves lucky because you have the choice to take the sling off; Joyce doesn't.

Just before my visit ended Pauline showed me around a bit more, she showed me the Christmas cards they do, the paintings that have been done. In general she showed me the pieces of craft that have been done by the people at the centre. Then we came to another cupboard, which she opened and guess what was in there: Him. *He* was in there. I was a bit surprised but I felt fine. I told Jo and Deb about this. They asked how I felt and I told them it was a bit of a shock but I was cool about it, I had no problem with it.

Well, me and Jo left the day centre and thought it had gone well. Jo asked how I felt. I explained that it felt good to have taken this nerve-racking step in my rehab, but I knew I'd feel more nervous when I actually went there on my first day to work.

# CHAPTER
# Eighteen

SO, MY FIRST day had arrived. How was I feeling? Nervous. How nervous? Very nervous. I kept telling myself, 'Come on now, Derek, you've had one hell of a seventeen months with the haemorrhage, moving, marriage and of course expelling a massive part of your life, Him; you can easily go into the centre and feel comfortable.' I kept telling myself this all the way to the centre. He did enter my mind but He was no way near as overpowering as He used to be. This had been my most noticeable round yet; He was still in the fight but surly now He could only win by a knockout?

As I walked into the centre the constant telling myself of what I'd been through brought a sort of calm over me and I knew that if I could get through the initial hour or so I'd be fine. I say the first hour because I'd planned it in my head that I'd go around for that time and introduce myself properly to the 'old dears' and get an insight into what had happened to them and explain to them why I was there. I knew that once I'd got the basic outline of their disability I'd be fine, because I think two of my best attributes are not being afraid to ask people any sort of questions and listening to people. I also knew where these people were coming from, so that was an added advantage.

I was also there to help serve lunch, tea, coffee and so on, and so on, but I can honestly say that I didn't and still haven't done much of that, firstly because I still haven't got the confidence to do things like that and secondly because there are so many interesting people to talk to, people like little Joyce who have had to contend with disability for most of their lives.

As you can probably tell, Joyce is my favourite, and even though you may think I shouldn't have a favourite I have, and I think all of the workers there have a favourite.

Well, when I got there Janice said ask Pat (another volunteer) if she wanted me to do anything or go and introduce myself properly and talk to the people. I asked Pat and she said just take the biscuit tin around and offer them. She told me who the diabetic people were and said they have a separate bicky tin. There were only three people for diabetic biscuits, but with my nerves and poor short-term memory it took about five minutes for me to remember the three people who were diabetic. I also almost dropped the biscuit tin because of my estranged left arm. You may be thinking, 'Yeah so what? Big deal!' Well, to me it *was* a big deal because I had no confidence; my confidence; was at it's lowest ever. In fact, on a scale of 0–100, my confidence was minus 100. I needed nothing to go wrong, not even the stupidest of things. I know that things will go wrong in the future, but by then I will have built my confidence back up again so that I will be prepared for almost anything.

Anyway, with the biscuit duty done I decided it was time to talk to some of the old dears and guess who I headed for first? Yep, you probably got it: Joyce. Because of what Joyce had been through and because I could relate to it and because she was the one who stuck in my mind after my first visit to the lodge, I wanted to find out more about her and how she had coped all those years with her disability.

Well, bless little Joyce, she gave me some photos to look at of when she was younger before the haemorrhage (right looker) and told me about her marriage (now divorced) and her children. She told me how it was mainly her who taught herself to walk and talk again. Now that is bloody amazing. I could never imagine trying to do that. In fact, I could never imagine a speech therapist teaching me to talk again. People have said how well I have taken the haemorrhage and all the physio and so on, but I know for sure that I wouldn't have handled it half as well as I have if I'd had to learn to talk properly again, *no way*. Another hard thing with a haemorrhage is that your short-term memory gets shot to pieces, which is very annoying. I myself have indifferent days, some good some bad; the main problem with mine is that I may be sitting down at the computer like I am now and thinking what to write when within a second it's gone, the piece I was going to write has popped out of my head, which believe me is well annoying, but with Joyce it's even worse because she can't even remember the names of her grandchildren, now how annoying must that be?

Well, I spent the majority of that first day talking to Joyce, which I found absolutely fascinating and good for my confidence. Janice said to me that I could come in every Monday plus another day if I wanted, so I said I'd come in Thursdays as well.

Now even though I'd taken that huge first step of going in that Monday, I now had another step to take because different people go in on a Thursday, so in a way I had the same nerves on my first Thursday that I'd had on the first Monday.

I got there and nervously said to another volunteer who I was and why I was there and got quite a shock because all the old dears were sat there with *Him*. I was certainly taken aback, because the last thing I expected to see was a load of old dears jollying it up with Him. I stayed composed and blocked out any temptation, which I have to say was quite easy, because at the end of the day if I ever was to go back to Him I wasn't going to be stupid enough to do it out in the open. Even when I was offered a glass of wine or an apple juice I plumped for the apple juice. Jesus Christ, years ago I would have gone for the glass of wine and said, 'Leave the bottle,' which, incidentally, reminds me of another story about my ex-wife. I'm sorry for deviating so much, but stories just pop into my mind as I'm writing.

Anyway, before me and my ex got married we were looking for somewhere to go on honeymoon. We didn't have much money so it had to be something cheap; in fact our money situation was so bad we didn't even have enough to go to a pub and get a couple of drinks, which even though I was at the early stages of my alcoholism was bad news for me. Well, just to give you an idea of what alcoholism is like, as we were walking round Bournemouth city centre we popped into Mark's and Spencer's – don't know why and probably didn't care why, because all I had on my mind was Him all I wanted was to fuel my body with Him so as to take the boredom of walking around Bournemouth away. Well, my boredom was soon taken away because inside Mark's and Spencer's was every alcoholic's dream: free wine tasting. I'll tell you what, my mood changed from boredom to excitement within a second as I walked around like a connoisseur, sampling every wine available more than once. What we had landed on here was like a little gold mine to it and me; certainty made the rest of the day more enjoyable for me. Even though I knew the next day would be filled with more boredom, it didn't matter because I was just enjoying the precious moments I had with Him. Now let's get back to the rest of the book.

So here I am on my first Thursday. There's different people, different old dears and different volunteers and I think I must have done more actual work in the first hour of that Thursday than I'd done in my previous Monday, but I still managed to get around and talk to some of the old dears. The major difference between Thursday and Monday, apart from alcohol being on show, is that on Thursday there's no little Joyce there, and as we know I do spend a lot of my time on Monday speaking to Joyce, but that's not to say I ignore everybody else there, because I don't and I have now got to know a lot more interesting people there. People such as Margaret (born stiff), Glenda (stroke), Ziggy, who was on the eastern front in the Second World War (stroke), Peter (stroke), Tony (Down's Syndrome), Barry (multiple sclerosis), Rosie (stroke), Lee, who's around the same age as me (torn ligaments), Phyllis (don't know yet), Adrian (don't know yet). These are just the people from Mondays. I haven't really got to know Thursday's people yet, as I've only been once, but I will get to know them.

As you can see, there're a few stroke victims and I find it fascinating to find out their experiences of the stroke and see how they compare with mine. Oh, and there's also

Betty, a volunteer worker, whose daughter has a friend around the same age as me who also had a stroke. Betty keeps me up to date about how her daughter's friend is doing and asks me questions about my experience, which I like; I like people asking questions about the stroke because it shows a genuine interest.

As you can see, I've got to know a few people since starting and it is certainty building my confidence up more and more, which is excellent because soon things will be moving to the final stages of my rehab, in fact those stages have arrived already.

Yes, I am now in the final stages of my rehab. I have had a meeting at the Job Centre with a getting back to work disability advisor, who was extremely helpful. She explained all the different options that are open to me and assured me that I would get all the help that I needed, which believe me is very reassuring when you have absolutely no idea of what you want to do. The woman (Carole Pritchard) gave me an information pack of what she had explained and basically said, 'Take your time and I'll hear from you again sometime,' which was excellent because it meant that I was in total control, and I must admit for the first time I felt in total control; I, not Him or anybody else was in control of me; my confidence was growing, I was getting stronger and I would now be ready for new challenges in my life, except there was a problem and quite a big one because I still had no idea of what I wanted to do. Come to think of it, I had no clue of what I could do. In my ideal world I would have just loved it to be able to walk into my ideal job with no application form or interview but hey, wouldn't we all love that?

Anyway, I read through the information pack and came across information about college; now college is something that originally I didn't want to do, but on reading the package the thought of doing a course became more attractive to me.

I read through the package and thought, *Yeah excellent, this is how I wanted it.* It was just me reading through a college package with nobody looking over my shoulder and saying, 'Ooh, blah, blah, blah that sounds like a good course you'd enjoy that.' If that had happened the whole college idea would've gone out of the window, because I was the one in control, nobody else. Anyway, one of the courses I was interested in was a carer's course. I think I was interested in caring for the shear fact that over the past year I had been cared for myself, so in a way I had some hands-on experience, if you know what I mean. Thing was, though, there was a problem with caring because I didn't want to do the sort of caring where you have to do toilet duties and so on; the sort of caring I wanted to do was where you go to an old dear's house and talk to them, make them coffee and tea, read the newspaper to them, do a bit of light shopping duties and so on, in general be some company for them. There may be an opportunity to do some caring like this and I would love to do it, but as my second choice, because on looking through the courses I came across what will be the ideal course for me if what people have said about me is true, which I am starting to believe myself, the things about being a good communicator, a good listener being able to put people at ease and so on and so on. Yeah, the course I have set my mind on hoping to lead to employment is counselling.

## Derek Williams

Well, who'd have believed it, Derek Williams wanting to train to be a counsellor? Looking back on what has happened to me with alcohol and the stroke, wanting to become a counsellor certainly seems like an ideal road for me to go down. I must admit that I think I'd be quite good at it – I mean, not trying to blow my own trumpet, but I've been there, I've experienced an addiction; I know the low, desperate feelings an addict has; I know how that addiction is more important to you than anything else. I would love to become a counsellor; in fact, the more and more I think about it the more and more I want to become one. I really do think that I can help people who want or need it because I am an open talker and more importantly an open listener.

Sorry, getting carried away there, but it's true about the counselling. I'm not just talking about people with addictions, because I think I can help people who have gone through an experience or similar experience to mine (stroke). I certainly know that if I'd had counselling before all this happened to me I would have wanted to know that the counsellor had experienced what I had and just hadn't read it from some textbook. So with all the experiences I've had, I think my credentials to become a counsellor are pretty good; what do you think? So after all my constant thinking of what I could do for employment I have used my own bad experiences as a positive and am one hundred percent confident that this is the path I want to take.

Talking about counselling, the day had come where I'd get my first bit of counselling from ADAS.

Deb had asked me if I wanted her to come along. I said, 'Of course I do,' because OK, yeah, I may be the alcoholic and the counselling will be strictly for me, but at the end of the day Deb is as big a part of this as I am, isn't she? I didn't want her to come to every meeting just the first one so as to give me a bit of moral support and also so that she could have her mind put at ease and get a general idea of what would be occurring.

Well, we got to ADAS and I was to have a meeting with a woman called... um, um let me think a moment... No, damn it, can't remember, that's another occupational hazard of a stroke; I'm absolutely hopeless at remembering names. Anyway, this woman met us in the waiting room and asked if I'd like Deb to come into the meeting as well. I said, 'Yeah,' then this woman said, 'Well why don't you come in first of all on your own then your wife can come in later?' I said, 'OK, fine,' but I did think what was the point in asking that question in the first place, do you know what I mean?

This woman started off by saying she'd get a general idea of my drink problem and then I'd have a meeting with a key worker who'd be assigned to me. This woman asked how much I drank, what I drank, did I drink alone or openly and when was the last time I had a drink. I answered all of those questions and then realised that the way the conversation was going this woman was under the impression that I was still drinking, so I explained to her the situation about the haemorrhage and that I'd only had about six pints in the last eighteen months. She explained to me that I was much further ahead in my rehabilitation than the people she normally deals with and that she really couldn't help me, but there was a bloke there who ran a relapse group and that would be the best thing for me to go to. Luckily enough, this bloke was in the building and he came and saw me. He asked me the same questions as the woman and said that the group was every Wednesday from 11.30 to 1.00 p.m. depending on how the flow of conversation goes. I said that I'd come along but in the back of my mind though, *Do I really need this, do I really need a bunch of alkies hugging and congratulating each other because they haven't had a drink in so long?* because as far as I was concerned I'd got my own problem under control. Then this bloke said that what the group aims for is that the members have complete abstinence from alcohol.

Now this got me thinking a little bit, because like I said, even though I'd got my addiction under control I thought to myself, *Can I really go the rest of my life without even a sip of alcohol?* Personally I don't think that I could, because even though I've come on in leaps and bounds in controlling my addiction, the rest of my life without any alcohol doesn't sound very attractive to me. I mean, how far do you take total abstinence? Do you do as a woman (Val) who I used to work at Don Giovanni's with does and not even have it in any of her food? Well, I suppose it's down to the individual, and me myself couldn't do it for the rest of my life.

Remember me saying that if I had a counsellor I'd want to know that that person had been through the same experience? I asked this bloke but he just said, 'That's something I may tell you at a later date,' which to me means yes. Well, I decided I would go on the Wednesday just to give it a try, I mean I had nothing to lose, did I? I'll talk about that in a bit, because another thing that was offered to me at ADAS was free acupuncture, yeah I was offered free

*Return Ticket Please*

acupuncture. Why? Well, it is said that in this day and age of unconventional remedies that acupuncture is supposed to aid and give a calming relief to someone who is trying to get off an addiction. Now whether this is true or not I don't know, but it would have been fascinating to find out. I'm not sure whether I would've given it a go, not because of the thought of needles being put in your ears but because to have a treatment like acupuncture done you are admitting to yourself and the whole world that you have a problem, and a serious one at that. Basically, the thought of having needles put into me wouldn't have bothered me, but my secret being exposed would have. Well, at the stage I am now I don't think that I would benefit anything from acupuncture and there is also a risk of doing acupuncture on me, as I am epileptic.

Anyway, I said a bit earlier that I was going to go to the relapse group they held on Wednesdays. Well, Wednesday was here and in all my years of alcohol abuse this was to be my first experience of any sort of alcohol group and I was blind as to what to expect.

I got there and thought there would be more people there than were because the turnout for this group was me, another bloke, a woman and the bloke who runs the group. I was a bit nervous but called upon my experiences of what had happened over the past eighteen months and the fact that these people had a similar problem to me to help calm my nerves.

The bloke who runs the group went through a few ground rules with me and then proceeded to ask the woman what sort of week she'd had. This woman explained what had happened over the past week, and by the sounds of it she'd had a pretty bad week because she had turned back to Him in a moment of weakness. Her husband had gone back to work and her daughter back to school and with the boredom of loneliness she turned to Him for comfort, which is something I fully understand, having been in that position in the past. She then went on to explain about wanting to go back to work but because of what had happened in her previous job her confidence had been shot to pieces, hence why she started drinking. I didn't get the full story on her previous job but by the sounds of things her ex-boss had belittled her so much that it crushed her confidence so much that there only seemed one option open to her and that was to turn to Him for that much-needed confidence booster, which as we all know He can give to us at our lowest point. I could associate with what this woman was saying, having been there myself, and I listened intently to what she was saying and I remember thinking to myself that this woman must have been quite confident to be coming to ADAS in the first place, because it was something I'd never, ever had the confidence to do while I was drinking.

Up to this point I hadn't said anything, but on listening to her talking about her lack of confidence in finding or even going back to work I used the experiences I'd encountered in all my rehab and asked her if, as I have done, she had considered doing voluntary work. I said to her that I could understand where she was coming from with her lack of confidence thing and said to her that in doing my voluntary work it was really helping me to build up my confidence again. I explained to her that in doing voluntary work you have no pressure and you get to meet new people who can boost your confidence up by just talking to you. She said she liked the sound of it and realised the advantages of it because not only do you have the reasons I've mentioned before but you also have the fact that you will be getting out of a lonely, boring home, thus reducing the risk of His temptation. Whether she does it or not is obviously her choice, but I must admit that I felt good drawing on my experiences and making a suggestion to someone who is without a doubt at a very low point in her life.

Another thing that made me feel good about it was the fact that this was the line of employment I'd be looking to go into in the future, so I suppose me being there more than anything else was to gain some hands-on experience on the counselling side of things.

After this woman had finished the bloke came to me and asked me to introduce myself and if I'd drank that week. I introduced myself and said I hadn't had a drink and then proceeded to say that in a way (small way) I felt luckier than the other two people there, because with me I'd been forced into stopping drinking because of the haemorrhage; yeah, it was a horrible way to be forced into it, but nevertheless a way it was. I then told them how I'd only drunk about six pints in the last eighteen months: A, because of what had happened to me; and B, because my life had been so busy with hospital visits, physio and occupational therapy; basically my mind had been occupied. I then told them that now was a time coming up in my life where I'd be vulnerable because now things were nearing the work side of things, which meant normality and normality meant boredom. The bloke then asked about my old drinking habits and was it drink that caused the haemorrhage. I told him how the people at Salisbury District Hospital had put the haemorrhage down to binge drinking, to which he said, 'So your drinking was a Friday, Saturday thing?' To which I answered, 'No, it was a 24/7 thing.' I told him about how I went along with the binge drinking theory because no one wants to admit their problem, to which the other two at the group agreed.

Anyway, the group ended and in just being there on my first visit I'd seen how far I'd come in my battle against Him, but it also made me realise something else, and that was something that would make me think twice about going again…

# CHAPTER
# Nineteen

WELL, THE THING that made me think again was the fact that one of the other ones there had slipped up; yeah, during the week this person had relapsed and gone back to Him because of her loneliness. When she was telling us about her struggle and how she was phoning up her family and friends just for the fact that she'd been drinking it hit me that, 'Yeah, I used to do that, yeah, when I felt lonely and had been fuelled by Him I'd phone up people just to release myself from the loneliness and boredom, and believe me this phoning up of people was just down to Him because I know for sure that I wouldn't have done it without Him.'

Then this woman also said that when she did all this phoning around of family and friends they knew she was drinking and I thought to myself, *Help her*. I thought, *Why doesn't one of her family or friends go around and see her? Why, if they know she's going to be alone therefore meaning she's going to turn to Him, don't they arrange to go around, maybe even arrange to stay a night or two?* You see, it's not just a counsellor who can help an addict; family and friends are just as, if not more, important than a counsellor. Even if this woman keeps slipping back into drink and you get annoyed and want to wash your hands of them, *don't*. This person has a very serious disease and is not slipping back into old ways for a laugh; she's not meaning to upset family and friends, it is one of, if not the, hardest thing I've experienced trying to kick a habit, but remember it's not sympathy she needs, it's help; she needs her confidence boosted when she is sober not when she's half-cut, because nobody needs their confidence boosted when they're half-cut because when we're half-cut we're all the best at everything, our confidence level is one hundred percent higher than when we're sober.

Well, I don't know the full story and maybe people have offered to go and stay with her but she has refused, preferring just to stay in His company. If this is the case, be patient and don't wash your hands of her because the more her confidence is boosted by going to ADAS then the more perceptive to people she will become, because don't forget if you've been an alcoholic for a few years it's hard knowing that you're alone and just yourself. You shouldn't worry about what people think of you, but everybody does, and believe me, it's a hundred times worse for a dry alcoholic.

Anyway, I was debating whether to go back to ADAS or not. Why? Well, after the piece I've just written about helping this woman and wanting to go into counselling you're probably going to think I'm a right hypocrite. After hearing this woman's story about relapsing I thought to myself, *When you're an alcoholic you are number one*. Did I need this, after coming so far, did I need to hear stories about relapse? Did I need to hear stories about how easy it is to go back to Him, because when I heard this woman's story the first thing I thought was, *Wow, this woman's turned back to Him and hasn't got bollocked she has just unscrewed the lid and tasted Him and made it sound so easy.* I thought to myself, *There are only three of us in the group, what happens when the group is bigger and there are more stories of people who have relapsed?* I don't know why, but for some naïve reason I thought that the other people in the group would have been at the same stage as me and wouldn't have a 24/7 struggle with Him. Now how naïve is that, but like I said, when you're an alcoholic you do just tend to think of your own struggles against Him.

Having written this bit you're probably thinking to yourselves, 'Well he hardly sounds an ideal candidate for a counsellor, does he? I mean, he can't even go to a relapse group and hear about people's problems; so how the hell does he expect to become a counsellor?' The simple answer to that is that I *want* to become one. I have listened to what people have said about my good points, which has boosted my confidence for the first time that I can remember. My confidence is boosted and I'm sober, so with my boosted confidence and clear head I know that I can do it. I mean, just because I give up on going to a relapse group it doesn't mean I can't become one, does it? The group would definitely give me some good experience for counselling, but would it give me the right type of experience? By this I mean would the counselling I want to do be based around a group or would it be one-on-one? I can tell you for sure the type of counselling I would want to do would be one-on-one, the reason for this being commitment, because to me if a person goes for counselling then they need the counsellor to be one hundred per cent committed to them. This is something you wouldn't get in a group counselling session. Don't get me wrong, people definitely benefit from these group sessions, but I personally think that you'd benefit more from one-on-one sessions. I know that I would, but as they say, it's each to their own, isn't it?

I do also think – and I'm not trying to sound arrogant here – that in my own mind I am a stage further ahead of the others that were there, obviously because of what had happened. What I understood of what they were saying was that their struggle against Him is an everyday thing, whereas my struggle doesn't happen as frequently, and if I do start to think about Him, well I've got my bad experience to draw on and steer me away from His advances.

Just quickly, one of the things I have kept from hospital to remind me of how bad I was is a photograph of me when I was in Southampton. My God, if ever I felt a really, really, really bad urge to go back to Him, all I'd have to do would be to look at this photograph. Christ, did I look bad. Anyway, that is just one thing I can draw on to help me through a crisis; the other people at the group may have nothing to draw on, hence why they go to the group, that group is their salvation.

Anyway, all this talk about me going into counselling is all very good, but I can't just become one overnight, can I? No matter what experiences I've had I'm going to need proper training, aren't I? I'm looking to take that first step into counselling by enrolling on a college course starting in January 2005. It will be then and only then that I'll find out if I am for counselling or if indeed counselling is for me.

# CHAPTER
## Twenty

I'M COMING TO the end of this book, and I must admit that I'm quite surprised at how much I can remember about my life, Him and the stroke. These are memories that will stay with me for ever, they will never be banished from my mind. In fact, as I'm sat here now more memories come to m. A quick couple are of the times I used to sit in my bedsit, just me and Him in front of the TV watching *The Full Monty* or *Braveheart* on video having thrown another sickie at work. Yeah, we'd just be sat there watching these two films, fast-forwarding to the parts of the film we liked best, never being out of each other's sight except for maybe when I wanted some food, which wasn't often because let's face it, He was my food; in fact, He was everything.

Looking back on it they were lonely times but I didn't feel lonely or at least don't think I did, because all the company I wanted or in fact needed was there with me.

Another memory was of me trying to substitute Him with a substance called kava kava. This was a herbal substance from the pepper plant which I'd read about in a Sunday magazine; what I could make out from what I read was that kava kava was like alcohol; it made you feel relaxed, happy, giggly; you know, all the things that alcohol gives you, except with kava kava you're not putting your body through torturous hell. Well, after reading about it I thought I had to give this a go, which indeed I did, but the only trouble was that I was never sober long enough, if at all, before trying it so I never knew if my exceptionally good moods were down to kava kava or just down to Him. You see, I was never brave enough to do anything without Him, the only reason I'd step out of the front door without Him inside me would be to stock up on Him, and as I was very meticulous in my planning of how much I had or required of Him that was hardly ever, if at all.

So, with what I've written does this sound a lonely life to you? Maybe it does, maybe it doesn't, but just being sat here writing this makes me feel it was. It also makes me think it's been a wasted life, although having said that I cannot deny that I've had some cracking laughs with Him and He's got me through some tough situations which who knows how I'd have handled without Him.

I'm going to just break off from my writing for a bit and put in this piece that Deb said to me the other night, which I thought was worded really well and also reminded me that I'm not the only one with this problem.

> Although Derek doesn't think shandy is alcohol I do, and when he drinks it he is still being fed by Him. Although it may just be keeping Him silent there's a chance He may start making noises again and rear his ugly head.

You see, when you hear something like that said by your wife it really does hammer home the truth and seriousness of this problem. Is it a problem that I'll have for ever? Well, I could talk about alcohol until I'm blue in the face but why, what would be the point? I've been asked by people if in writing this does it make me feel better – you know, does it feel good to get all this off my chest? I've answered, 'Yes, it does make me feel better,' but if I really sit back and think about it, no, it doesn't, because just in writing this down doesn't mean He's gone, does it? I mean, let's face it, alcoholism will be with me for the rest of my life, won't it? Even if I didn't drink for ten years it'd still be there. I know you hear people say, 'I was an alcoholic and now I've been dry for ten years I've recovered,' but to that I say, 'No, no you haven't recovered you haven't got the flu, you just can't take a couple of Lemsips and be cured, you've got a disease not an illness, and diseases can't be cured, diseases are slowed down, diseases are put in a dormant state, you're not ever going to be cured of a disease.' This may sound like a very defeatist attitude, but it is how I feel, and once again is only my humble opinion, but come on, if you think about it if something really bad happened to one of these supposed cured alcoholics what would they do? Who would they turn to? Would they have the inner strength to resist His temptation or would they do as I know I would and turn to Him for that support that is needed in a very bad situation? I'm not going to spell out what a very bad situation is, just safe to say that it isn't losing your job, being in debt and so on, and so on, it's… well, I'll just let you work it out for yourselves.

So, in writing this does it mean that at some point in my life I will go back to Him? If it does and I do it will mean that after being so far ahead on points in the biggest fight of my life He KO-ed me in the last round. I know that I will always have the support of my family and friends and my life is getting back on track, but in the back of my mind I do have a massive hole in my life, a hole that was once filled by Him. I will always be classified as an alcoholic; it's a stigma I'll have to live with, but it's a stigma that if He had got His way would have been a lot worse.